The Wedding Hacker

A Budget-Minded Planning Playbook

Heather Loree Fier

ISBN: 978-1-7336579-0-7
Published by Delphic Marketing LLC

Hand-drawn calligraphy and artsy touches by Sarah Fier,
www.instagram.com/sarahfierart

Gorgeous photography by Chasing Daylight Photography,
www.chasingdaylightphotography.com

Interior formatting by IndieDesignz.com

To the love of my life, my husband, Joe Fier. Thank you for teaching me to live each day to the fullest. I am so thankful for the beautiful life that we are creating together.

In memory of Grandad, Jack Bennett. I know you are loving that I'm sharing the JB method with the world and remembering to save my pennies, eat dessert first, and have fun every day.

Table of Contents

Preface

I wrote the first words in this book over four years prior to finishing the final sentence. After my initial burst of excitement, this project sat dormant, untouched for well over three years. This book came back to life after a poignant discussion with a bride-to-be.

The pressure of the wedding industry, her family, and her social circle to spend more and create an over-the-top romantic event was sending her into an anxious tailspin. She and her fiance wanted to elope and save for a new home, but she told me she was "not allowed".

This grown woman in her mid-30's who was paying for her own wedding was telling me that she was "not allowed" to have the wedding she truly wanted.

This broke my heart.

I decided to move forward on this project with the aim to inspire couples to release themselves from wedding obligations, rules and outdated traditions suffocating them. Couples are getting married later in life and more often paying for their weddings themselves. A wedding is their celebration of love and should be what they want and can afford.

Starting out your married life buried in debt to appease family, friends or your Instagram followers is absolutely unnecessary. You can achieve your wedding dreams without breaking the bank.

Couples can pick and choose the "hacks" that fit with their wedding priorities and budget. Spend big on the items that bring you joy and fulfill your wedding vision; enlist the budget-minded strategies for the aspects of the day that are less important to you.

Writing this book has been an adventure, I want to express my gratitude to friends and family who have listened as I excitedly shared the progress on this book.

Special thanks to those who contributed to the book with their artistic eye. Sarah Fier, my talented sister-in-law, for creating the vision for the cover art and the handwritten calligraphy throughout the book. Thanks for all your time and effort on this project!

Deep gratitude to Kate Mills of Chasing Daylight Photography for contributing her gorgeous images to this book. It has been a joy watching your business grow over the years! Thank you!

Thanks to other vendors who have added to the vision of this book through long discussions about the needs of budget-minded couples. This book is a bit contrarian, pushing back against the boundaries, rules, and pressure placed on couples by the wedding industry. I truly appreciate the vendors who have supported this vision alongside me.

Many thanks to all the friends and family members who encouraged me to chase after my dreams over the years—I am grateful for all of you.

Other photographers featured in this book include: Blue 22 Photography, Analisa Joy Photography, The Rasers, Kelsey Becker Photography, SD Photo Studio and True Photography. It has been a pleasure working with all of you over the years.

May this book brings hope to couples who have been told that their wedding vision is impossible. You've got this!

Keep joy and fun in the wedding planning process; that is what this whole thing is about after all.

Enjoy the journey!

Heather Loree Fier
December 2018

Weddings
do not need
to be expensive.

There is an enormous amount of marketing in the wedding industry to shake extra money out of couples' pockets. This book will help you let go of the pressure to spend big on your wedding day and walk you step by step through the planning process.

The very real truth is that a wedding that costs far less than the "average" American wedding can be *your* dream wedding. Depending on the environment you are in, the term *budget wedding* might mean spending hundreds, thousands, or tens of thousands of dollars. The wedding mecca, TheKnot.com, estimates that the average wedding in 2017 costs $33,391. This number is overinflated and heavily marketed in order to add to the societal pressure for you to spend more.

The 13,000 couples who participated in The Knot's "research survey" did not represent a true cross-section of the near 2.5 million weddings that occurred in the US in 2017. They did not even have a single respondent from twenty of the US states; the responses received represented only 0.5 percent of the weddings that occurred in 2017 in the US. The data was intrinsically biased, as only couples who follow the site and voluntarily provided details on their budget were included and created a precedent that weddings have to be expensive.

Do not buy into the pressure to spend on pace with this contrived image of what an "average" wedding looks like. Facing the reality of this societal pressure to spend big is necessary for you to let it go so you can focus on your own vision of an amazing wedding day. No matter how large or small your budget is, this book will provide some out-of-the-box thinking that will help your event come together beautifully. I've provided recommendations and advice that was collected from couples across the country who maximized their wedding budgets to the fullest extent.

If you have the bankroll to plan a $100K wedding celebration for your family and friends, more power to you. For most of us, any large chunk of money sitting around would more wisely be used in a much different way. If you are reading this book, you likely don't have access to a briefcase full of cash. Or perhaps you are planning on using your money in another way with better returns. If so, good on ya!

If saving your hard-earned money isn't enough inspiration to rein in your wedding day spending, consider a recent study by two professors at Emory University, which revealed couples with smaller wedding budgets have longer marriages. Starting your marriage without the heavy burden of debt and putting your focus on your relationship rather than your wedding will help lay a strong foundation for years to come.

This playbook will help you develop a clear vision of what you *really* want from your special day, and then we will dive into a long list of hacks to help you plan it within your budget. We will run through the standard categories of expenses for a wedding and look at ways to optimize each expense by thinking outside of the box. Some of the "hacks" recommended in this book veer far from the traditional, and others stay pretty close to the path with just a slight twist. Depending on your wedding day vision, you can pick your own adventure, selecting the tips and tricks that will work best for you.

My ultimate goal is to help support and empower couples to have the day of their dreams on the budgets of their realities. No matter your budget, this playbook should help guide you to stretch what you do have as far as you can. With a bit of creativity and ingenuity, be confident that you can have a beautiful wedding day without breaking the bank.

Good, Fast, or Cheap

(pick 2)

I want to set an expectation for the reality of planning a wedding on a budget. Without the cash to pay professional vendors to take on the brunt of the workload, this process is going to take some extra time, effort, and creativity.

A budget wedding will take more time and effort to plan than a wedding with a higher price tag. Either you need to be open to putting in the work or you will need to pay someone else to put in the effort on your behalf. Let me cut it to you straight—if you are tight on both *money and time*, then you may need to adjust your expectations or vision of your wedding.

Adjusting your expectations does not mean you can only have an elopement (although that is a totally valid and lovely option covered in this book). It might mean a smaller guest list, less traditional format or location, or trimming away a lot of the "nice-to-haves" that do not inspire you.

In all most things in life, one finds that we can have good quality, we can have it fast (a.k.a. with minimal effort), or we can have it for cheap. We are only able to select two of these three options. We have to sacrifice one of the attributes to secure the other two. You have the ability to pick: *good and fast, good and cheap,* or *fast and cheap.*

If you have a limitless budget, you could secure the very top vendors to pull together the day of your dreams. You would able to select *good* and *fast* (a.k.a. minimal effort). You would be paying for someone else to expedite the work in a professional fashion. Some might feel frustrated that vendors charge what they do. I've heard couples complain about the high price tag associated with the hottest florist or calligraphy expert in town, but there is no reason to rail on these folks.

Professional vendors provide amazing service and have refined their skills in their selected crafts. They are experts and do their jobs very well, so they deserve to be paid fairly for their work. These vendors will take your vision and, with minimal effort from you, execute your big day flawlessly. Why should they cheapen themselves? Their craft takes time, developed skills, and a lot of effort. If there are couples able to afford these services, kudos to them. The reality is that not everyone has the deep pockets to pay someone else to do the work. But just because that is the case, this does NOT mean there is no way of building the wedding day you dream of.

So are you going to pick FAST or Good?

Since achieving your budget goal is a high priority (maybe even the highest priority) for your wedding day, we know you are picking *cheap*. If using the term cheap is making you uncomfortable, take a breath. The wedding industry has made it a dirty word; cheap for some implies low quality, but that is not how I am using it here, and I encourage you to reframe this word in your mind. See the definition below and own this type of cheap for your day!

Cheap /CHēp/
Adjective
1. (of an item for sale) low in price; worth more than its cost.

synonyms	inexpensive, low-priced, low-cost, economical, competitive, affordable, reasonable, reasonably priced, budget, economy, bargain, downmarket, cut-rate, reduced, discounted

I am proud of my ability to secure an awesome deal on something; to me, it is a well-crafted skill to be able to make something happen for the best price without losing quality along the way. My husband is often embarrassed when I respond to a compliment about new shoes with a detailed breakdown of my savings on the item. This is just part of who I am, and I am proud of it (and deep down I know he loves my spendthrift nature). If this means I am labeled *cheap* and banished from the wedding industry, so be it. I hope I can at least help a lot of couples before they kick me out of the clubhouse.

This playbook is primarily angled toward the couple who wants a wedding that is *cheap and good*.

This means that I am assuming that:

- You want a wedding that feels like it costs much more than it actually did.
- You may want many of the traditional wedding touches.
- You are aiming to get the most for the money you have without sacrificing *your* vision for the day.

If this is in alignment with your wedding goals, you will find a treasure trove of ideas in this book.

If you just are aiming for a *fast and cheap* wedding, this book may have a bit more information than you really need. You can snag some vendor savings tips from this book and then head down the aisle. Fast and cheap is a totally valid option, which can be pulled together in a very special and memorable way. You'll find a chapter at the end of the book with some ideas targeted to your goals; they all align with a vision of an elopement (local or destination) more than a traditional wedding. If you go this route, you can always plan a wedding celebration with friends and family using ideas in this playbook as well.

Because the majority of you are aiming for *good and cheap*, this book will give you guidance and tools to help keep your planning headed in that specific direction.

BUILD IT *and* *let it go*

Let's take a moment to talk about your emotional state as you plan your big day. The truth is that there will likely be some challenging moments ahead. How you react to the challenges along the way will make or break your wedding planning experience.

The stress of pulling together a big event is undeniable. A research study found being an event planner is the sixth most stressful job. My opinion why event planning is so stressful is because planners ultimately have to give up control of the thing they created. Planners build visions, get organized, make decisions, and then need to let go of it. In the same way as your wedding nears, you have to trust others to take the event across the finish line.

Reserve a little time each week to work on your wedding planning, and before you know it, the plans will come together in a beautiful way. You will be ready to hand off the project to others, so you can sit back and enjoy. This is a very special time in your life, so make this planning journey fun. Have a crafting night to prepare decorations with friends and family. Test out first dance songs in your living room for a romantic date night. There is no reason you can't find joy in each step of the planning process.

This is a playbook, and it is meant to be interactive. Feel free to make notes, highlight helpful points, cross out points you won't use, and really use this as a planning tool. Through the coming pages, I will be asking the key questions that I would ask my full-service event planning clients. These questions are checkpoints on which you can reflect regarding your progress and make sure the big day you are planning is still in alignment with your vision.

Let's get started with the vision for your *good and cheap* wedding day!

OWNING YOUR VISION

Before jumping in and choosing a venue, booking a caterer, and buying decorations, you need to begin by visualizing in detail what you want from this event. Creating a wildly successful event begins with a clear vision.

Take a minute or two and visualize your perfect wedding day. Make note of what you see, hear, smell, taste, and feel. What aspects of the day jump out at you and hold a high value to you? Have your partner do this visualization as well, and make notes about your wedding day dreams on the open space provided or your wedding planning notebook.

What does your PERFECT wedding look like?

You cannot plan the wedding of your dreams without first figuring out what you want to accomplish from the event. For many, this first step can be a challenge. Maybe you have no idea what your dream event would look like? Maybe you have *helpful* friends or relatives adding to your stress by pushing their vision of a wedding? Or possibly you are so overwhelmed with ideas and inspiration from magazines, books, and websites that you have no clear vision of what you truly want?

With the overabundance of wedding ideas on social media and the thousands of images of Martha Stewart perfect parties, it is no wonder that many folks have given up before they even start planning. The world bombards us with what great weddings look like and sets the standards so high that many are intimidated. You need to take some time to sort out what you want from this special day. One amazing resource that I recommend to the couple feeling overwhelmed as they work through the planning process is the Bridechilla Podcast. The episodes are funny, sassy, and stress-relieving; it can truly help keep your wedding vision grounded in reality and provide a sense of community on the sometimes lonely road of wedding planning.

Now is the time to really tap into yourself and what you and your future spouse love about a wedding. As the wedding couple, you set the tone and the vision and move forward with that vision steadfast as the destination point. Think about any weddings or events that you have attended as a reference point, as you can likely pick out aspects that you loved, hated, or simply didn't notice at all.

The key questions that you need to ask yourself about your wedding vision are:

1. What feelings do you want the guests to have at the event?
2. What is the goal of the event?
3. What is your budget for this event?
4. If you had to pick the top three aspects) of the event that are most important to you, what would they be? (An example might be food, photography, and music.)

The answers to these four questions are at the heart of your day. These answers will help guide the development of your day. If you stay connected with these answers throughout the planning process, you will be able to stay on the path to *your perfect wedding day*.

Every single celebration is unique and keeping that in mind will allow you to avoid a huge amount of unnecessary worry and stress. Comparing your wedding to another, even to another wedding of the same budget, is helpful but can be anxiety-inducing. We don't want that—we want a joyful planning experience. Your wedding is a celebration of your love and should be uniquely you. Be true to what you love and the day will come together much more smoothly.

If you and your love are foodies, then that should be reflected in the event. Do you love to camp or enjoy art galleries? Those are great places to build from. Building the vision for the event from part of your personality or hobby makes for a much more special and intimate day, as opposed to a generic run-of-the mill wedding with no connection to the couple. Some of the most memorable weddings that I have been a part of went far from the well-worn wedding planning path, including out into the dunes of the Southern California desert. SD Photo Studios captured the day beautifully; it was a day that was truly in perfect alignment with this amazing, desert-loving couple. They are a perfect example of building your wedding around your interests and lifestyle.

It is good to research and look for wedding inspiration a little, but do so with caution. Staying in research mode once you develop your vision for the day can be very problematic for a budget. New ideas and inspiration will strike, and suddenly your budget balloons as the event grows and morphs. Over time, an event can grow from a simple cocktail hour with appetizers and an open bar to a formal, plated dinner with a DJ, photo booth, ice sculpture swans, a mariachi band, carriage rides, and a two-story chocolate fountain. That sounds like one wild party but one that will definitely cost far more than the intended budget.

Getting inspiration and ideas from other weddings is wonderful and necessary, but just keep in mind *what is really important to you*. Keep changes and growth in the event's structure in check. Sometimes more is fabulous, but other times more is complicated, unnecessary, and expensive.

Knowing what your true purpose and goals are for your event will help you stay focused on *your* definition of success. For some hosts, a truly magnificent event must include ornate flower arrangements, gourmet hors d'oeuvres, and a wine selection that would amaze the finest sommelier. That is totally fine and doable on a budget, but it will mean keeping those priorities in mind and dialing back in other areas of the event.

As the wedding develops, some changes are natural and some flexibility will be needed, but staying true to the plan will keep your budget and vision in check. As you move ahead with planning, your priorities should be reflected in how you allocate funds. Go big on the priority items, and go more budget on the areas that are a low priority.

Handling *the* Numbers
(Wedding Budgets 101)

The most common wedding goal of couples is for their guests to have an amazing, memorable night. If your goal is along these lines, it is safe to say breaking your budget is never necessary. Think back on the most special moments in your life. I would place a big bet that the people and the energy in the air made it special rather than the price of the meal or the outfit you were wearing. These factors can add to the fun, but they are never going to make or break the memory of a special moment.

I have assisted with weddings that cost about $1,000 that were extremely fun and reflected the couple's style; there was an aura of sweetness and love filling the room. I have also attended events that cost in excess of $100,000 that felt rather cold, unwelcoming, and sterile. Years after an event, guests will not remember the flowers or if there were handmade party favors; they will remember the way they felt at your event.

The experience and feeling of your wedding are really lifelong gifts you will give to your guests. If you are not concerned about this, I want you to check in on why you are having a traditional wedding at all. A traditional wedding is a party you host so your guests can celebrate this special moment with you. If you just want stunning photos of a gorgeous ceremony with dreamy florals and don't prioritize the guest experience or their involvement in the day, then consider the elopement options outlined later in this book. There is nothing wrong with this at all, your priorities are just out of alignment with this type of event; let yourself create the event you really want.

Creating a lovely guest experience does not have to be an expensive feat; you can find the same feeling in a venue at a high-end hotel ballroom or by renting (or borrowing) a large house for a weekend. A budget hurdle that some couples face is the input of friends and family. I am not going to tell you to ignore (all) of these people. Obviously, these people are important to you. If they are not paying for the event, they are not in the position to pressure you into burying yourself in debt to plan *their perfect wedding*. Be gracious when (unsolicited) opinions are provided and continue to develop an event that works for you. People who love you will still love you no matter what your wedding day looks like.

There is a caveat. Problems arise when couples don't communicate well with each other and their friends and family. If your future mother-in-law requests to invite thirty of her friends to your wedding but there is no way to accommodate that in the budget, be honest. Tell her you would love to make that happen, but it is not possible due to the budget constraints. Maybe she will offer to add in some money or maybe she can host a small wedding celebration for her circle after the wedding to celebrate. Communication that is direct and comes from the heart will help get through these hurdles without unnecessary drama.

If other people are contributing to your wedding day, having these conversations will likely be extremely more important. They may have expectations for your wedding and if they are contributing toward the event, you want to make sure everyone is on the same page. Before you start spending the money, make sure you understand all the stipulations and red tape. It is better to be clear on what you are really agreeing to before you deposit a check with loads of strings attached.

For many people, admitting that the wedding budget is tight or discussing a wedding budget at all will feel uncomfortable. Financial situations are often awkward to discuss, but this is not the time to let an uncomfortable feeling stop a conversation. You are hurting yourself by overextending your budget to avoid an awkward chat.

By putting a small spin on the situation, you can have the discussion without saying outright that you and your future spouse are "broke" (even if that may be the situation). You can say that you are prioritizing your goal to buy a house or invest in your future and you are aiming to be true to a reasonable budget. Having these tough conversations in a calm way will set you up for successful planning without outside forces continually pushing you to max out your credit cards.

BUDGET BREAKER : Contracts and Hidden Fees

One of the biggest problems that cause a budget to blow up on a couple is the fine print in a contract. Before locking in a vendor, let me stress how important it is to read any contracts in detail. There can be a lot of hidden costs in the fine print that will hit your budget hard—delivery fees, cleaning fees, service fees, damage fees, etc.

Here is an example of how much the fine print can impact your budget. A friend of mine once planned a two-day event at a hotel for his company; the hotel estimated his costs at just under $17,000 for the venue. When he received a final invoice for *$28,000* after the event; he was shocked. Clearly, he missed some major details in the fine print. There were many add-ons to the base cost of the room that the hotel's special events staff did not mention would cost extra.

- Did he want water bottles for the event? They did not mention those premium bottles that cost $7 per unit.
- Did he want a variety of soda for his guests? *Those were $5 each.*
- Did he want to use the hotel's tables? *Those were $10 each per day, plus linens ($12 each), plus laundering fees ($5 each)*

On a different occasion, while planning a wedding for a young couple, I scouted a lovely location that advertised a fabulous deal of $1,500 for the event space, tables, linens, and chairs. The venue did require food and beverage be purchased through them for a reasonably priced meal at $39 per person++ (plus tax, plus gratuity).

At first glance, the event for eighty people, would cost about $4,000 for food and beverage and seemed to be within the couple's budget. Upon reviewing the fine print of the venue's contract, it was clear that the venue would not work. The *minimum food and beverage order was $12,000* no matter the number of guests. The total cost would have been $13,500 minimum for the venue, food, and beverage plus tax, service fee, and gratuity. This would have been more than the total the couple had budgeted for their whole wedding day.

It is very common for couples to ask about the additional fees on their proposal that increased the cost from the listed $59 per guest to over $100 per guest.

Let's do a quick lesson on event planning math and break down some of the terms you will likely see on your contract.

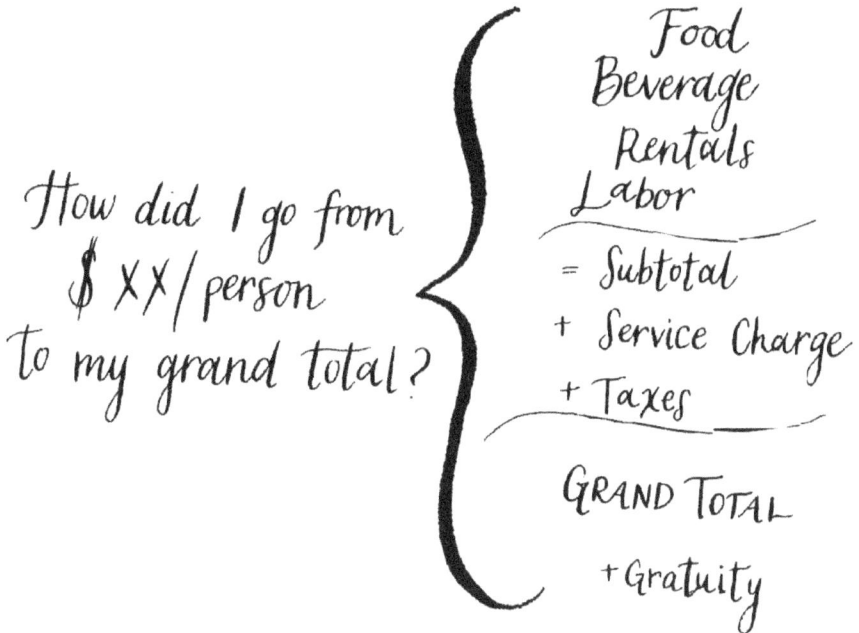

How did I go from $ XX/person to my grand total? {

Food
Beverage
Rentals
Labor
―――――
= Subtotal
+ Service Charge
+ Taxes
―――――
GRAND TOTAL
+ Gratuity

++: When this is listed after a price, you need to do some math. "Plus, plus" signifies that the price listed does not include the service charge and tax. You will want to do a quick calculation to get the approximate final cost per person

Service fee: A service fee (or event production fee) is an obligatory charge added to your venue and/or catering contract. This is NOT the gratuity. This is a cost that was likely listed in the fine print of the pricing you initially reviewed when selecting this vendor. The service fee will often be a percentage of your total bill, but can also be a set flat rate in some cases. The service fee covers costs for the vendor that are inherent to doing business, such as event labor, overhead and administrative time.

Gratuity: Just as you would provide a tip after a wonderful meal, you will want to tip the servers and bartenders at your wedding. Confirm that gratuity is not included in the invoice automatically; some companies will include it on the final invoice or provide a line on the final invoice for you to fill in the amount you'd like to provide. Gratuity is customary with many wedding vendors; having a trusted family member or friend pass out thank you notes including cash tips in sealed at the end of the reception is a great way to show gratitude.

Sales Tax: The sales tax varies by city and state and is generally calculated from the subtotal, including the food, beverage and service fee.

Depending on the venue's rules, the ++ after a price could add between 30-50 percent more to the total final invoice. Request that the estimate to include ALL fees, taxes and suggested gratuity so that you are not shocked by the final bill. No one wants to deal with a surprisingly large expense on their wedding day. Remember to plan for the gratuity for vendors, as most will never list it on their estimate. Check out this vendors tipping guide for details on who to tip and how much is customary. Just because you are having a budget wedding does not mean you can disregard tips for your vendors; plan it into the budget because those traditionally earning gratuities often depend on them. Your affordable wedding does not come at the expense of others' livelihood.

Vendors and Budget Concerns

There are many event budget templates online which can be useful in getting organized in the early planning stages. While I think the recommended percentages that are given on these templates are helpful, these numbers should be adjusted based on *your priorities and goals*. I find that there are often entire categories that some couples can drop from the list once they reflect on their vision.

Many of these expenses are based on the traditional structure of a wedding. With the modern technologies available, spending in certain categories can be reduced significantly. For example, it may not be necessary to pay for the creation, printing, and postage for save-the-date cards and formal invitations. Many hosts now utilize an event website, online RSVPs, and an online invitation. This can save hundreds of dollars or thousands with little to no impact on the guest experience of the event.

Another way to save big on your budget is to bundle costs. Finding a DJ, band or venue that provides the audio/video equipment and some snazzy lighting can help minimize costs and simplify your planning. Many professional DJs offer lighting and special A/V equipment for a small additional fee; dealing with one fewer vendor makes coordinating the event much simpler and streamline the event set-up process.

Finding great, reliable vendors is something that many hosts struggle with when planning a big event; this is actually one of the big reason that many folks hire an event planner. They are looking for an expert to help them find reliable and professional vendors. Event planners can be an amazing resource, but sometimes they recommend vendors based on personal preference, referral fees, or long-standing relationships, so it might not always be the most unbiased or budget-minded advice. When keeping on a budget is your priority, no one will care more about that goal than you and your future spouse.

21

Again, I want to state that professional wedding vendors truly deserve what they charge for a high-quality service. Vendors work hard to develop their skills, brand, and company to earn their premium rates. There are many, many hours worked before or after your event to provide you the final product. Vendors work diligently to make your day amazing. This book does not discount the value of the amazing services they offer, but I am going to say that you do not need to feel pressured to hire one of these companies if your budget will not allow for it.

With current technology, you do not need an expert to locate a great vendor. The internet is an enormous resource in finding amazing people to help on your big day. There are many well-known websites—Yelp, Thumbtack, Wedding Wire, Bark, and Gigmaster. All of these sites allow clients to give feedback and rate their experiences. Personally, I prefer Thumbtack and Gigmaster because they allow you to receive bids from vendors while still factoring in their history of success. There are catering companies, photographers, videographers, entertainers and many more vendors listed on all of these big name websites. They are a great starting place and help keep your resources targeted to your local area.

Another really helpful resource is your personal network, did your friend or cousin or friend's cousin just got married in the area you are holding your wedding? Ask who they used, what their experience was like and what they paid for the service. If it sounds in alignment with your needs, reach out and mentioned that your friend referred you; it will start the relationship off on a good note. If you don't know anyone personally, check Facebook for local wedding planning group for resources. The Wedding Hacker Facebook Group is an awesome resource where you can connect with other budget-minded couples to locate the best deals in your area. All members of the group prioritize their budget, so there is no judgment and lots of support and resources available.

The most affordable option for most vendors it to get creative with the four B's—*beg, borrow, build or barter*. I'll get into this in details as we cover each vendor category with more specific ideas. Here are some quick examples of outside of the box thinking that can save a lot of money without much extra effort.

- Forget about renting linen for an overinflated price, buy them used from a wedding resale site … and you can resell them after your wedding for the same price.
- Rather than hiring a DJ, ask your outgoing cousin to play the MC in lieu of a gift. Pull together a playlist and select the songs for the big moments. With detailed instructions and a timeline of the reception, things can flow beautifully.
- Scratch renting an arbor for your ceremony, build one with your sweetie. Use it in your backyard for years to come or resell it to another couple.
- Don't buy floral displays for every table, borrow some beautiful succulent arrangements or greenery from a local nursery for the weekend.
- Rather than paying for your cake in cash, perhaps you or your future spouse have a helpful skill to offer the bakery. Can you make them a new website? Help them paint a mural? Spend a day organizing their garage?

These are just a few ideas, but they all show that with creativity and a little effort, you can dramatically reduce costs. I love to see couples come up with win-win that allow them to secure vendors at no or low cost. There is a benefit in the deal for everyone in these scenarios; no one has to "lose" in order for you to have a budget-friendly wedding.

That said, let's take a look at the traditional breakdown of wedding costs. Depending on the style, locations, and size of wedding you are planning, these percentages can vary greatly. The ranges on the infographic should give you a starting place, but depending on your priorities for your event, you may drop whole expense categories or double down on other categories. We will dig deeper into the breakdown for a wedding budget in a later chapter.

Wedding Expenses BY CATEGORY

Venue (CEREMONY/RECEPTION) 10-30%

Food & Service 30%

Beverage 5-15%

Photographer and/or **Videographer** 10-30%

Tables, Linens, Décor Rental 2-5%

Table Settings 1-2%

Dessert 3-5%

Decorations & Floral 5-10%

Lighting 0-3%

Entertainment/Music 0-10%

Audio/Video Equipment 0-5%

Dance Floor Rental 0-3%

Favors 2-5%

Escort Cards/Place Cards 0-2%

Programs 0-2%

Menu Cards 0-2%

Save-the-dates & Invitations 1-4%

Thank-You Notes 0-2%

Postage 1-3%

Shuttles/Special Transportation 5-10%

Valet OR **Self-Parking Fees** 0-2%

Totally Flexible Costs

Wedding Rings (Bride & Groom)

Officiant Fee/Donation

Gifts FOR Out of Town Guests

Corsages AND Boutonniers Ring Pillow

Bouquets for Bride, Bridesmaids, Flower girl

Veil AND Bridal Accessories

Tux/ Suit Rental

Groom's Accessories

Bridal Gown

Gifts for Bridal Party

Many of these expense categories are optional. Feel free to cross out any category that does not add to your wedding vision. With the mindset of *beg, borrow, build or barter*, you can find ways to minimize a lot of these expense categories.

There are numerous online tools to keep your budget on track throughout the planning process (see a great article detailing available budgeting tools here). The Knot's budgeter is great for keeping expenses organized, but the system is built to sell you on vendors advertising with the company. TheKnot.com wedding budgeter, like most wedding industry tools, do not work super well when planning a budget wedding. The system suggests vendors in the area and even the most inexpensive suggestions will break a budget of $20K very quickly.

If you are going to use this tool or others like it, be aware that they are produced not only to help and inspire you but to also encourage you to spend more with the vendors in their advertising network. The Knot and others are still very helpful resources which can provide inspiration and amazing, free wedding planning tools; just realize that finding a venue or any other vendor suited to a budget under $20K on these sites will be a true challenge. To find the budget-friendly gems, you need to explore your local community, network, and resources.

Wedding Guestlist:

Developing your rough guest list is absolutely necessary in order to select a venue. If you book a venue before digging into the guest list, there is likely to be more frustration and potentially hurt feelings. Before moving ahead and touring venues, get clear on your needs. Sit down with your future spouse and start making a list. I recommend categorizing guests into these groups

1. Must be there (top tier)—You can not imagine getting married without these people present on your big day.
2. Would love to be there (second tier)—You would love to have this them at the wedding, but would not be sad if they were not able to attend
3. Would be fun to be there (third tier)—You would like to have them at the wedding, if possible.

Work with your love to come up with a full list of guests. If you are receiving money to fund the wedding from your parents or another relative, then you should offer that they invite a few guests as well. I recommend taking your time with this step. Keep a notepad with you for a week and jot down a name when it comes to you. The people in the top category will be very obvious to most couples, but tier 2 and tier 3 get a little more challenging.

Many couples are very anxious about excluding people from their guest list. I can tell you from my personal experience that over the last decade, very few couples regret their decision to have a small wedding. In fact, if my husband and I were to do it again, I would probably cut the guest list down by half to make the event even more intimate.

Very few people who were not invited ever asked about it and when that issue comes up, simply express that you want an intimate event and the venue would only accommodate a small number of guests. Approaching the issue with love is enough to defuse the situation without any drama or resentment. Do not be afraid to make tough calls on the guest list. Just be prepared to discuss it with openness, honesty, and love; true friends will be understanding and want good for you, your budget, and your special day.

Once you feel like you've dialed in your invite list, you can estimate your venue needs. Research shows that 83 percent of guests RSVP yes to attend a wedding when it is a local event. If you have 100 people on your list, then you can estimate that about eighty-three will attend. If you are worried that your guest list is too big for your budget, don't panic. We can work on developing an affordable plan for you as we move ahead and you are not sending invites yet, so nothing is set in stone.

When you are preparing invitations (months from now) and you are worried that your venue might feel overpacked, you can stagger mailing invitations which will drop the RSVP rate down to closer to seventy-five percent. Send out the top-tier invites twelve weeks before the wedding, tier two invites out ten weeks before the wedding and tier three invites out eight weeks before the wedding. With each round of invitations, the RSVP rate will drop a little lower as folks fill up their calendar with other obligations.

Once you've dialed in your guest list, prepare that over the coming months there will be a ten percent increase to that list. As you see friends and family and are asked about your engagement, it can be difficult to hold the line and not feel like you should add more people to the invite list. Check in with yourself on how your personality will hold up to these potentially uncomfortable moments. Having an accurate estimate of your number of guests is very important before you start seriously looking at venues.

MISSION CRITICAL : *Venue Selection*

enue selection is the single most critical decision for your budget. There are innumerable gorgeous backdrops for a wedding in this world. Seriously, there are gorgeous and meaningful venue options all over the place, but it can be hard to spot these with all the marketing overwhelming our senses.

If you search "wedding venues near me" on Google, you will see many options to consider. With your budget as your top priority, I would recommend immediately ruling most of these venues out. Any location heavily marketing itself as a wedding venue on popular mainstream wedding hubs will be charging couples a premium, have loads of fees in the fine print and most likely a narrow list of preferred vendors. It is possible to find a deal at one of these wedding venues. Perhaps they will give you a lower rate for a Friday or Sunday wedding, but that will still not fix the requirement to use their preferred vendors.

Selecting the right venue saves you money on the venue, but most importantly it opens the door to save money with all the other vendors you book. Take time searching and selecting a venue, your effort will pay off big dividends as the planning continues.

If you have already found a wedding venue that you absolutely love and they have a lot of limiting rules and regulations or a higher price point, stay calm; put on your poker face and get ready to negotiate. Be flexible on the timing (think off-season), time of the day, and day of the week. The venue might be open to better pricing options based on taking a date that they might not book otherwise. If the pricing has no flexibility, aim to negotiate in some flexibility regarding vendors that will bring other costs down. Here are some key points to negotiate into the venue contract.

1. Vendor Options

You want total flexibility on vendors. If the venue has a short list of allowed vendors, you may end up forced to use a vendor that is overpriced and under delivers. Any time a venue has preferred vendors, the vendors are loyal to the venue, not you; the venue will connect them with work long term and they know you have no options, so they are less motivated to work with you on price or deliver exceptional service. Caterers are the vendor most commonly preset in a venue's contract and happen to be one of the most expensive vendors. If a venue has a preferred caterer (or vendor) list, ask if you can use other vendors with proof of insurance and the venue's preapproval.

2. Alcohol

Assuming you are not having a dry wedding, alcohol is an expense category is heavily impacted by venue rules. Often, venues have their own bartending team and pricing for wine, beer, and cocktails on a per beverage or per guest/per hour. The best case scenario for your budget would be that the venue will allow you to purchase alcohol for the event yourself and hire a certified bartender to serve. If you love a venue and the bar policy will break the budget, you do have some options which I'll discuss later in the book.

3.   On-site Rentals

Some venues include your basic rentals in the cost of using the room. This is very convenient and budget-friendly, but sometimes the items available will not suit your taste, so ask to see the items. It is common for venues to provide tables, chairs, and linens for a reception space, as well as chairs for a ceremony space. If a venue does not include these items, this is just something to factor into your planning, as deliveries for rentals are tricky to coordinate and can be costly.

Assuming you have not found a venue that you are set on, the first step in picking the perfect venue is answering two key questions:

- What sort of space fits with your wedding vision? Indoor, outdoor, rustic, formal, bohemian, eclectic, etc.
- How many people will you invite?

Beyond your vision and the size of the venue, consider what sort of venue would work best for your guests. You want to keep the comfort and safety of your guests in mind, so if you have twenty children on the invite list, a wedding on a steep cliffside is not ideal. The venues that will not work for your budget, vision, and guest list can be crossed off quickly, no need to force a venue. There are so many of options out there, so be confident that you will find the right location for your wedding.

One other key question to reflect on before you can select a venue is **when do you want to get married?**

I would recommend booking the venue (for reception and ceremony) about nine to twelve months in advance, but you can always book something out further. To maximize your budget, I would research venues beginning around twelve months out from your approximate wedding date. I would aim to secure the venues around nine months before your wedding day. Booking too far in advance will work in favor of the venue—they know they have time to book another couple, so they may not be flexible on price or adjustments to the contract.

Planning a wedding for in less of nine months is not impossible, but definitely not recommended if you are busy with other aspects of life. There is actually a good chance you will save by having a shorter engagement, since many vendors offer specials for "last minute" bookings within the next six months. Most people mail invites about two to three months before the wedding, so technically, you could book the wedding four months out, but just be prepared for a more intense wedding planning experience if it is so compacted.

To have maximum leverage when negotiating with your venue, I would recommend being flexible on the wedding day/date. Getting married during wedding off-season will allow you the most room to negotiate with all vendors; target dates when vendors are slower and more eager to take any work they can (even at a discounted rate). Considering a Friday or Sunday wedding is another way to save a bundle when planning a wedding; pairing up a Friday or Sunday wedding with a long, holiday weekend—can give you the upper hand with pricing. Your guests will likely have time off work, so it is a win for everyone.

My husband and I got married the Saturday after Thanksgiving and it was perfect for us. The venue had no other wedding all weekend, so we had access to the venue for set-up and break down the day before and after the celebration. We found amazing vendors and negotiated pricing that worked for our tiny budget. Almost all our family was in attendance since they were available for the holiday weekend celebration. I really encourage couples to be flexible because the opportunities that open up can truly be amazing.

Before touring dozens of traditional wedding venues, take some time to think outside of the wedding industry box. Brainstorm a list of places you'd have access to that might work within your personal network.

- Do you have a friend or family member who has a large yard or home? Maybe they would be willing to allow you to use their space for a small fee? Or as a wedding gift?

- If you are open to an outdoor ceremony, research your city, county, and state parks locally. Many public spaces can be rented for events—parks, beaches, & other city facilities. Often the fee for reserving these venues are very small compared to a similar space that is professionally marketed as a wedding venue. There is generally a simple permit application process and a small fee due when booking these sites. Note that the fee is generally cheapest for a resident of the city, so consider using your aunt Susie's address if she lives down the road from the park you are hoping to reserve.

- Make a list of the top ten places you like to eat that would have an aesthetic that would work for your event. On that list, there will likely be about half that do not specialize in or market themselves as a space for an event. Call those restaurants and speak to the general manager because it is likely that a few of them would be willing to allow you to reserve a room or the full restaurant for your event if you hit a minimum spend on food and beverages. Often this type of deal is much more affordable than a traditional "wedding venue". Rather than paying for a room… and food … and beverages, you get the room for free for buying the food and beverage. It is a saving for you and a win for the venue because they have a guarantee of income for the day of the event.

- Is there a part of town that you'd love to have the reception in, maybe there is a hip area with cool, funky backdrops for photos. Take a day to walk the area and explore. Maybe there is a community center for a local HOA or a warehouse space that is not used on the weekends? Finding a space that the owner is not using for events, but could be is a great option. If you make them an offer to rent it for a small fee for a twenty-four period for your event and let them know you will secure event insurance, it is a huge win for them since their space would otherwise sit empty.

- Churches are traditional venues that can often be affordable options and the amount paid for the venue is often tax deductible since it is considered a nonprofit donation. For members of a church, the venue for the ceremony and reception can be very affordable and convenient.

- If you like the idea of holding the event at a private home, but you don't have access to a home you would find suitable, check online. VRBO and Airbnb do have homes that can be rented for events. These homes will often be available for three or four day minimum rentals, so that needs to be factored in. If there is nothing available there, contact some local real estate agents and tell them what you are looking to do. They might have a gorgeous, vacant home that the owner is willing to rent for a day or two.

Getting creative and thinking outside of the traditional wedding venues will result in a much more unique celebration. Personally, finding a private home to rent is what I've found to be the most cost-effective. You can host both the ceremony and wedding on site. There are no rules or limitations on vendors. You can stock your own bar. You can design the space to suit your needs and guests personality far beyond the limits of any traditional wedding venue.

Finding these gems can be tough since they are often not heavily marketed; the best deals really do come from personal connections, so tap your network before starting your research of more traditional venues. With the peer-to-peer movement online, more off-beat venues are popping up all the time. If you are looking for venue inspirations, I recommend exploring Peerspace, Unique Venues, EVENTup, Wedding-Spot.com, Splacer, and VenueBook. Some of these sites only cover a few big cities, but browsing the venues available might inspire you to reconsider the beauty of your aunt's art studio, cousin's garden or best friend's HOA community center.

If you select a venue that is off the beaten wedding path, be sure to cover your liability with wedding insurance. Many traditional venues require proof of insurance, but even if it is not required, you will still want to secure a policy since it protects you in the case there is an injury or property damage. If you will have friends and family assisting with set up instead of professional vendors, wedding insurance will also cover your liability during set-up and breakdown.

Wedding day liability insurance can be secured very easily online and is not a huge expense. Check out WedSafe one of the leading wedding insurance providers. When you secure a policy, confirm it includes coverage for alcohol-related incidents, as well as the rehearsal dinner, ceremony, and reception. Taking this precaution is a smart step and allows you to protect yourself no matter where you decide to celebrate on your wedding day.

Now is your time! Go get creative and go hunt for an awesome venue for your wedding day… once you have secured a venue, then you will continue on to the next phase, vendor selection.

Real Wedding Case Study

⤜⟶⦿⟵⤛

Kelli and Seth

Sept 17, 2016

Singing Hills, CA

⤜⟶⦿⟵⤛

Kelli and Seth prioritized the perfect venue, fun for all guests and photography on their wedding day. Kelli was determined to secure a venue that would not only be beautiful for their wedding day but could also host out of town guests. She wisely steered away from hotels and traditional venues in order to find a space suited to their budget.

After a lot of searching, she secured a private home with a lovely, large yard as the event venue. Kelli said that finding a homeowner open to allowing a wedding ceremony and reception on the property was challenging but well worth the effort.

The couple opted to skip one big tradition which allowed for significant savings and freedom with their planning—no wedding party. Without bridesmaids and groomsmen, they saved on bouquets and bouts, gifts, makeup and hair styling, and wardrobe. It also just simplified everything. Kelli noted that their close friends were still very involved in the event, but they were free to come and go and just relax.

Seth and Kelli leveraged the accommodations at the venue to host some out of town friends who doubled as vendors. The couple paid for a flight for a photographer friend who lived out of town who gifted them wedding photography.

Another friend went to the flower market with Kelli and helped create DIY floral arrangements. Kelli said that those who arrived days before the wedding had lots of fun preparing for the wedding together.

If they were to do it again, they would have planned out a more detailed schedule for photography to allow for a smoother portrait session with friends and family. They also wish they had some raw drone footage of the wedding.

Overall, they loved their wedding day and were happy that they held to their vision and budget.

Food, Beverages, & Sweets

I am not going to lie. I love food. Personally, I am extremely disappointed when I'm at a wedding lacking delicious food options. To me, food and beverages are the most important aspect of the guest experience, so I would never sacrifice on flavor to keep on a budget, nor does one need to.

Food, beverage, and sweets generally total up to be one of the biggest expenses for a wedding. This makes sense as a wedding reception is essentially a meal to celebrate your marriage. Keep in mind that the food and service charges will grow in proportion with the number of guests, so the first step to minimizing cost is to dial down the number of guests. We will take a look at some other options for you to consider to keep costs in this expense category suit your budget.

To stretch your cash, I recommend that you prioritize flavor over formality; a beautifully plated dry piece of chicken with rice is not going to make your guests giddy, but a full plate of delicious tacos from a food truck will. If you have an extremely tight budget, there is no shame in going with a much more casual approach to your celebratory meal. If you have a desire for more formality, then you may need to dial back the celebration from a meal to a cocktail and hors-d'oeuvres reception.

Assuming you made a wise decision with your venue selection, you should have a lot of flexibility with regard to the budget for your culinary vendors. I have found that guests are thrilled when the food at the wedding is something different than the basic catering cuisine. Don't get me wrong; when the standard catering selections are prepared well, the food can be amazing! There are caterers out there who serve the basics with flare and flavor, but they are rarely the budget-friendly companies. Generally, having some unique catering option is a more exciting experience for guests and a lot of the time it is much more affordable.

1. Rather than looking into regular catering companies, look a little off the beaten path and consider making the choice more personal.
2. What are you and your sweetie's favorite restaurants?
3. What is your favorite food?
4. Where did you go out to eat for your first date?
5. Where have you celebrated a special anniversary?

Anniversary date? Check into these places and see if they do catering for events. Having a story and a real reason for the food selected makes your first meal as a married couple even more special. If you find a restaurant that doesn't normally caterer but is willing to for some of their favorite customers, you will likely lock in a special "good guy" rate for your wedding.

Here are some culinary ideas to explore that I've seen in action at weddings that were mouth-watering and did not break the bank. If you select to go with one of these less formal food options, be sure to take a detailed inventory of the tabletop items you need to rent or acquire; these caterers may not have the formal polish of the higher priced meal options. These may not be foods people initially think of as "wedding food", but all of these foods have loads of flavor and will ensure your guests are not hungry. All of these options cost about $20 or less per person out the door (maybe $25 with fancy rentals to jazz up the look):

Tacos—In Southern California, there are a ton of street taco vendors who will come out and grill up killer tacos fresh at special events. Your guests will be happy to feast on Mexican goodness!

Pizza—Check your local farmer's market and you may just find a mobile woodfire pizza oven. The pizzas are often artisanally crafted, made to order and served fresh.

Crepes—Another unique option for the international foodie is a mobile crepe company. Savor crepes for dinner with a salad and a sweet crepe a few hours later for dessert.

BBQ—Catering from your favorite barbecue restaurant would be an amazing option for a casual outdoor wedding reception. Depending on the menu you select, you can keep the costs reasonable and delicious. Some grilled chicken would be an affordable option and a little (lot) cleaner than ribs.

Chinese—One of the most delicious and impressive meals that I've had at a wedding was a banquet of traditional Chinese food. The food was served family style at each table. The food added color and spice to the tables and the guests left the wedding with "to go" boxes.

Cuban—Cubano sandwich, black bean and rice, and plantains would make for one flavorful meal. Pair this food with a signature mojito on the bar menu and you will have a culinary backdrop for a long night of dancing under the moonlight!

These are all delicious food options to consider that have maximum flavor with minimal cost. With any of these affordable options, you can build out an amazing feast for your guests without the hefty cost of a more formal wedding caterer. Most of these options will give the flexibility to feed any of your guests—no matter their dietary concerns. I would recommend that you always add on a salad or vegetarian dish in some format to make sure all your guests find something that suits them on the menu.

Are you hoping for a more formal wedding while working with limited funds? If so, I would consider a cocktail reception only. By serving cocktails and heavy hors-d'oeuvres—think sliders, skewers, bacon wrapped dates, dips, cheese, crackers, and crudites vegetables—you will keep your guests happy and minimize a lot of costs since you aren't hosting a sit-down meal. You will want to provide some seating, but can offer belly bars and lounge seating, as opposed to traditional wedding tables. This will dial back the amount of decor and florals needed, as well as the space needed; you can hold a cocktail event in a significantly smaller venue. This style reception can be very glamorous, fun and maintain a high level of formality with tray passed appetizers.

If the options that I outlined are too much for your budget to handle, here are a few extremely low-cost options to consider. These options require a little more time and effort, but you will reap the financial savings.

1. Skip the full-service catering altogether. Order your menu from a local restaurant or store, pick it up and set up a lovely buffet for your guests. Without the staff to serve the food, you will likely need someone to keep an eye on the buffet to keep it tidy and well

stocked. You may need to rent or borrow some chafing dishes to keep foods warm for your guests.

2. One very fun, easy and economical option if you want to cut the catering cost way down is a "Spud Bar" paired with a salad and some grilled chicken kabobs. Bake a large number of potatoes to suit your number of guests (or whip them into mashed potatoes) and provide lots of fun toppings in a buffet format. Most of the preparations in the kitchen can be handled the day prior, to minimize wedding day stress. Your guests can fill up and your cost per guests will be a few dollars. Put a little effort into signage and cute serving bowls and this low budget buffet food option can impress. *I used this menu for my parent's thirtieth anniversary party and feed sixty guests for less than $4 per person.*

3. If you are working on a very, very tiny budget, consider a potluck. Many couples are resistant to this idea, as it does not fit the traditional vision of a wedding, but the truth is… it totally aligns with the spirit of a wedding day! Everyone is coming together to support the new couple in their commitment to each other. With a potluck, they are coming together with their contribution of food for the celebration. If you choose this option, then you should make it clear that you would love them to contribute a dish in lieu of a wedding gift.

Negotiating WITH *Preferred Vendors*

If your selected venue has a single preferred caterer or a tiny preferred vendor list, you will be a bit more limited on how you can save on catering. You will really need to lean into the *beg* and *barter* to keep within your budget.

Here is an outline of how I would approach negotiating and securing a caterer from a small preferred caterer list.

Step 1: Check the pricing for all the preferred caterers and request pricing and all the fine print. Is there a minimum? What are your most affordable options (that align with your vision)? Watch for extra fees that are not noted on the per person price list.

Step 2: Check the online reviews of the companies, so you can rule out any vendors that might be lackluster or unreliable.

Step 3: Take a personal inventory of what you or your future spouse can offer to negotiate. Going to the vendor and just asking for a discount is not likely to get you far. You need to find something to offer or barter. If you have skills they could use (web design, bookkeeping guidance or free labor), you might be able to negotiate a trade or partial trade to make the event worth their effort. My husband and I used this technique in our early days as entrepreneurs and managed to land trades for acupuncture service, free meals, and many other services/products.

Step 4: If you've got nothing to offer (unlikely … you've got to have some useful skill!) then consider negotiating to minimize costs. Rather than just asking for a discount, let the vendor know your budget goal and see what they propose to help reach that budget goal. You may have to go with a buffet meal rather than plated, or drop one side dish, or stick to a single meat dish. Keep calm and focus on finding a win-win for yourself and the caterer. If the vendor is eager to secure the event, they will likely work with you and a plan will come together.

Step 5: After negotiating with all the caterers that you were considering, select the caterer who best suits your needs and lock them in without delay. Get the contract inked and move on to other details. You can plan a tasting with the caterer closer to the event to finalize the menu details at that time.

Something Sweet

Traditional wedding cakes can be so gorgeous, delicious … and expensive! The average cost for a traditional cake for 100 guests is about $500 plus delivery plus cake cutting fee. To keep your cake from overrunning your budget, I've outlined a few pointers below.

- I love that couples are getting creative with their desserts at weddings. There are still a lot of traditional cakes, but I also see gelato, donuts, pies, and cookies regularly at receptions. Your guests will be happy with any sweet and you can save a budget by dropping the formal cake from the line-up.

- If you envision that special moment of cutting the cake with your spouse, avoid fondant. It looks beautiful but it costs a fortune since it is super labor intensive for the baker.

- Whatever size cake the baker recommends, order a cake between fifty and seventy-five percent of that size. This adjustment is dependent on whether other sweets will be available. I have never seen a whole wedding cake be eaten at a wedding. Guests are often too full to eat a full piece and many skip cake altogether. Most weddings end with a huge amount of cake packed up to go home with the couple or their family (or both). If ordering a smaller cake makes you nervous, buy some other little pastries to ensure you have ample treats for everyone.

- For maximum saving on the cake budget, get a beautiful single tiered wedding cake for display and ceremonial cutting. In the kitchen or catering area, have a sheet cake or two for the staff to cut and serve to guests. Sheet cakes will taste just as delicious but will be a fraction of the cost. You will have your special moment and photo-worthy cake without splurging. With this option, you may also avoid the bakery delivery fee since a single tier cake and sheet cakes are very easy to transport in comparison with a three tiered behemoth.

- Fine print alert! Most caterers charge a plating or cake cutting fee ($2-5 per person) to cut and serve the cake. This covers their staff's effort, plates, and flatware. Consider asking a friend or three to assist with cutting and serving the cake during the reception. You can purchase some high-quality disposable plates and forks and you'll avoid any extra work for the caterer's team.

Using these pointers, you can delight your guests with a decadent dessert for a fraction of the cost (under $100 is totally possible). While dialing in your budget and dessert selections, do not forget to schedule a cake tasting … after all, you deserve a treat! This is really one of the most fun vendors to test drive. While you really can't make a bad decision, you can have fun making the selection. Book the cake tasting as a fun little date with your love and get excited about your special day. This is a happy time, so don't miss out on these special moments.

Bartenders & Beverages

Depending on the number and type of guests attending your wedding, this is a budget category that can get very pricey if you don't set boundaries. The key money saving tip here is to pick your venue wisely. Some reception sites will allow you to bring in your own alcohol, mixers, soda, and just pay for their staff to serve. If you picked a venue with loads of flexibility on the bar situation, kudos to you!

If you did not, you will be ok and I really hope you love that venue (I am sure it is lovely). You will need to revisit the steps listed for negotiating with caterers earlier in this section. The bad news is that when venues restrict bartending companies, they most often select a single preferred company, so there really is not a lot of room to negotiate. If this is the case, just jump to step three and see if there is something you can offer in trade. If that isn't an option, then your most cost-effective option without fully scraping a bar altogether is to offer a cash bar.

On the note of skipping the bar altogether, I would recommend providing a cash bar at the minimum unless there is a really good reason to exclude it. If your family and your future spouse's family are all non drinkers and would be upset to be in the presence of drinking, it may be worth considering a dry wedding. If you don't drink or don't have the budget, you are not obligated to buy drinks for everyone all night, but forcing a dry wedding may frustrate a lot of people. Many of your guests will want to enjoy an adult beverage at the reception or at least to have the option to drink at your reception. The few weddings I've attended or coordinated without a bar in the reception space were impacted by that decision. The room clears out as soon as dinner finished and a sizable percentage of guests ended up across the hotel at the lobby bar.

For those of you who know you want to have a bar, here are some questions to ask yourself:

- What is the venue's rules on alcohol?

- Can you hire an individual who is a licensed bartender? Or do you need to use a bartending service?

- Do you really need(want) a fully stocked bar? Or could you provide just beer, wine, and a few signature cocktails?

If you are going with a cash bar, the company will likely provide a standard variety of beverages and you can recommend items you know are popular with your guests. There will likely be a bartender event fee ($500-1,000) which will cover the bartender's time (barware, set-up and break down) and the bar itself if the venue doesn't have one built in. Your guests will then pay for their drinks when they are ordered. If you go with this option, note this on the invite, so guests bring cash to cover their drinks.

If you have a little more bar budget to work with, you can offer an open bar during cocktail hour and then switch over to a cash bar. Another cash bar hybrid option would be offering wine at the tables for guests (maybe two bottles of wine and a bottle of champagne per table) and then a cash bar for additional drinks. Many venues will allow you to have wine or champagne set on the tables for a small corkage fee. I personally love this option because it minimizes the traffic at the bar. If you know that you have a large group of alcohol drinkers, consider having two bars on opposite ends of the venue to ensure that folks do not spend the whole event in line.

If you have the option to purchase alcohol to stock the bar yourself, kudos! This is a huge money saving option. You can coupon, watch for sales, tap friends for employee discounts and then stock up. Depending on your preferences and your guests' preferences, you have a large number of options. I do recommend keeping the bar as simple as possible. If you try to accommodate every single beverage preference, you will spend a fortune and end up with an enormous amount of alcohol to take home at the end of the event. I recommend offering two to three beers, two to four wines, and one to two signature mixed drink. This will dial in the shopping list and speed up the bar staff when serving guests without cutting into the fun.

If you want to offer alcohol for shots and sippers, then select mixed drinks that feature alcohol that can be served solo and just purchase extra alcohol to account for this. A Practical Wedding created an excellent resource on calculating your wedding alcohol needs and going into all the nitty gritty details of stocking your own bar here.

Mocktails

Just because these drinks are more innocent, doesn't mean that they aren't fun. One great way to minimize how much alcohol your guests drink during the event is to offer some snazzy non-alcoholic drinks. Stepping up the beverage option beyond the standard sodas will attract a more attention to these sans alcohol options and encourage your guests to pace themselves on the hard stuff. If you add some fun flair, guests will likely be curious and ask to try the special drink.

Depending on your wedding style, you can find some awesome fun and colorful beverage options to whip up. One big perk of this is that a signature mocktail will likely save you some money too. You can purchase ingredients in bulk and rather than aiming to stock every soda under the sun, you can make a special option and then provide one or two select other options. Not only will children and pregnant guests sing your praises, but you will also be happy when you tally up the beverage costs.

Check out these amazing and delicious recipes for mocktails from the OffbeatBride.com for inspiration and remember that the garnish and presentation can do a lot for inspiring guests to give a mocktail a try.

Bringing together your Style

*I*n the era of Pinterest, the style of an average wedding has been pushed to the next level. There is an endless catalog of wedding photos for inspiration online; it can be amazing for inspiring your wedding style and absolutely maddening as it can cause overwhelm. Having too many options to pick from can quickly cause analysis paralysis; the variety of great options makes it difficult to choose at all and you can't get any momentum going at all.

Once you get some momentum going, I would still proceed with caution on sites like Pinterest and Instagram; they can give so much inspiration that your budget explodes. Aiming to make your wedding look like the photo may literally be an impossible feat. Many wedding photos used in marketing materials are actually professionally staged inspiration shoots or "styled shoots" not real weddings; these staged photos are gorgeous and rich with style details and gorgeous florals but are often not achievable in reality without an enormous budget.

Professionals are heavily styling a single table or seating area in these photos in a way that will look amazing in a photo but would be completely impractical in reality. Take this gorgeous styled shoot from Green Wedding Shoes.

These images from Jason Mize Photography are so romantic and stunning, but in reality, this wedding would not work due to a number of issues. This biggest question I have is… How would your nana sit on that pillow for the whole ceremony?

The reality of wedding day logistics is very, very different than a styled shoot. There are a lot more moving parts on a wedding day, so be sure to keep your expectations in alignment with a *real* wedding. When you find the inspiration from these photos, be ready to get creative and execute the vision in a way to stretch your dollars and accommodate the logistical realities of an actual event.

These online platforms Pinterest and Instagram are bursting with beautiful wedding inspiration and you will certainly be able to find a style or feeling for your big day. There are many event stylists, planners and designers who bring will bring together the look of the event, but these services are generally rather expensive and will refer you to high-end vendors. They all offer incredible service, but with your budget in mind, you will likely need to find another way. If you are drooling over styled shoots and that is what you are hoping for your wedding day, see the elopement section at the end of the book for an interesting idea that might suit your heart's desire without breaking the bank.

Now that we are back to the reality of planning a real wedding, let's reflect on your style. When considering your style, you will be considering colors, textures, warmth and perhaps a theme. I recommend sticking to a color theme or set of tones rather than focusing heavily on a theme. A fabulous online resource to develop a color pallet is ColourLovers.com. You can play with different tones and shades until you land on something you and your future spouse love. There are many color pallets listed on the site created by others, so there is endless inspiration.

Depending on the formality and location of your wedding, varied color schemes are more suited than others. I personally recommend selecting at least one neutral color in your pallet. Neutrals would include shades of browns, whites, ivories, greys, black and metallic. These are common linen colors available with all rental companies, so you will likely find better economical options in these tones. Keep the metallics—gold, silver, bronze, and copper—in moderation for a little extra pop and fun. These are wonderful to weave into the event details.

Are you hoping for help dialing in your style? If you plan on booking rentals for your event, there are often stylists available as a resource at no cost. Many rental companies offer complimentary design service or a free "style board" to help you develop your vision. You can work with them to create a clear vision; be prepared to stay strong on holding to your budget. They are helping you for free, but they make money on renting you more items, so realize every little item they add to the tablescape has a cost. Shop around for the best pricing or dial in your order to include only items you could not source elsewhere for a better price. See the vendor section in this book for negotiating tips and tricks.

Having a theme for your wedding day can really tie things together and add some extra sparkle to a big day. I will also note that generally, *less is more* with regard to theme. You want the event to flow, but you don't want the event to look childish which is sometimes the feeling that comes with over-the-top themed weddings. For the budget minded planner, there is an extra benefit to the less is more approach since it will be more affordable, too. All the beautiful little details can start to add up, so being deliberate with a few key pieces to give a cohesive feeling to the event is the goal.

Once you decide on a theme and/or color pallet, it seems as if an endless supply of options appear that are *perfect* for your wedding when you dig online. Etsy and Pinterest searches can take you on a path that leads far from your budget goals. Take it easy and be strategic about placing a few key nods to your theme at the event. If you want a "love bird" theme for your wedding, tie in the invite, set a cute birdhouse out on the guestbook table, two birds atop the wedding cake and maybe bird shaped salt and pepper shakers on the tables. That's all you need. Your guests will get it and appreciate these themed items.

You do not need to continue the theme in every detail of the event. Honestly, it can become a little silly if you do; it pushes the details from cute to hoaky. If you put a bird on every details at the wedding, it is overwhelming and blurs together. *This is just my personal opinion and I've seen some beautiful events with the theme slapped on every detail. I can guarantee you that those events were not cheap and they would have been equally lovely if a few of the birds had flown away.*

At some point in the planning process, you need to check in with yourself and ask, "do I really need to spend my evenings for the next month hand carving bird shaped escort card holders?" Most likely, the answer is no. Planning an event is a delicate process and it is very easy for things to snowball; suddenly, the event is growing into something much larger, and more pricey, than you ever planned. Keep checking in as the event develops to make sure you are being realistic about your expectations.

If you have a vision of a gorgeous Pinterest-worthy bohemian wedding with high style, consider creating one highly styled focal point at the event. Maybe you go big on your sweetheart table or with a lounge cocktail area. You can carry out the vibe throughout the event with a much lighter level of styling to balance the budget for decor. This will allow you to have the look you want at your events and get some photos that you will love without your budget suffering.

Every inch of your event does not need heavy styling. Let yourself off the hook and remember that the photos you are looking at for inspiration are the highlight reel from a wedding; just because they are not showing you the tables with much simpler decor doesn't mean they weren't there.

All the Pretty Things

Oh my, how Pinterest and Instagram have impacted the wedding industry. The lovely, tiny details of a wedding have become the focus of the camera lens and the obsession of many brides and grooms. While I absolutely love design and am in awe of the craftsmanship, style, and beauty of many design touches, I will warn you that this expense category can blow up on you faster than any other. The expectation and reality are often miles (or tens of thousands of dollars) apart for couples dreaming of the blog-worthy wedding day.

The reality of many of the photos you see online is that they are staged photo shoots, collaborations of wedding vendors planned to inspire couples. Vendors come together with a shared a creative vision to set the stage and it photographes very well. The vendors are setting a scene that is romantic and perfectly styled, but not an actual event. There is a single, gorgeous table in an idyllic backdrop; the bride and groom are models. They styled the beautiful scene, but scaling that scene to effectively create a real wedding would be extremely costly and in some cases impossible.

With that in mind, if you are daydreaming about a funky, bohemian lounge or an eclectic mix of flatware for your table that you spotted in a magazine or on a blog, you will need to get a little creative. Your vision may need to be scaled back to a more realistic scope.

Rather than imagining every corner of the event looking picture perfect, realize that only key locations in the room need to be styled to perfection. With this in mind, you can develop your dream vibe and images for your scrapbook or social media profile.

The following aspects of your wedding are perfect for heavier styling because they are focal points that will be resilient to the wear and tear of hours of wedding fun.

Sweetheart or Head Table

This is often a centerpiece of the reception. There is more space for styling the tabletop since fewer people are seated here. Go with upgraded items that fulfill your Pinterest dreams to set this table apart or incorporate something significant or special to your relationship. True Photography captured these lovely ladies including something unique on their sweetheart table that reminded them that they are always a team.

Guestbook Table

If a larger table is used, you will have lots of room to add florals, photos and decorative details around the guestbook. This is a spot all guests should visit during the event, so allow it to make a statement.

Dessert Table

If you go for a traditional, tiered cake, I recommend it to be set up on a smaller table where it can be on center stage. If you go with a single tier cake, you can set it on a larger table with photos, flowers, and other decor items.

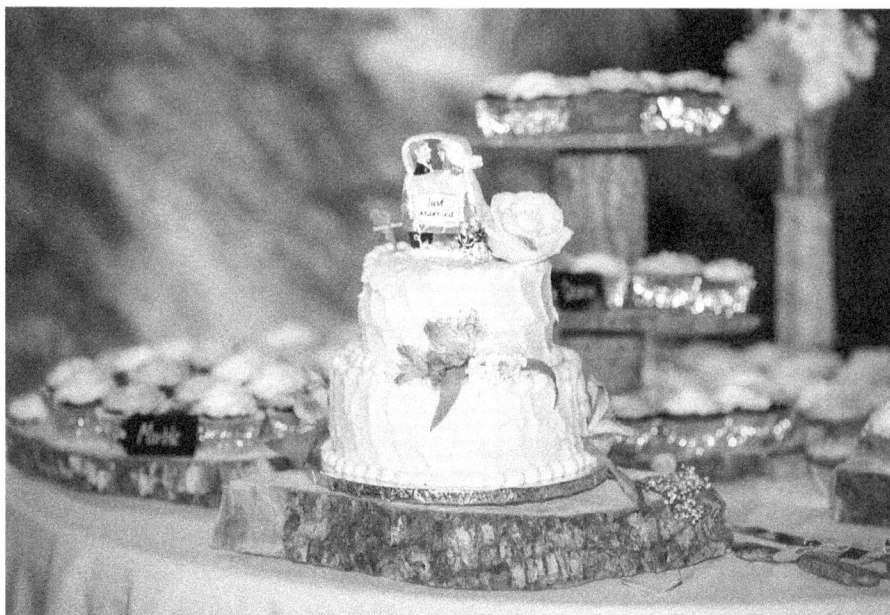

Family Photos, Memorial or Tribute Table

If you have a table to honor and remember friends, family, and successful marriages that came before you, consider decorating this table up a bit more since your guests will certainly enjoy the stroll down memory lane.

The Bar(s)

I would recommend a small to medium (depending on the size of the bar) floral display or decor item at the corner(s) of the bar. This will tie it in with the rest of the decorations. If there is not a bar built in, then you can really go wild.

Lounge/Cocktail Seating Area

If you want to set up a beautiful lounge area for your guests, it would be best to set it up near the bar. If you are opting for a heavy appetizer only reception, then you could expand the lounge style a bit more, but realize any money you saved on food might be eaten by your rental budget. Moving furniture is hard, so having rental furniture is either going to take some sweat from you and your crew or cost some significant cash to orchestrate.

Ceremony Altar

This is the center focus of the ceremony, so this is the spot to go big with the style you are envisioning. You do not need to spend a huge amount to achieve this, clusters of potted plants, a rug, two floral displays, or a more traditional (mandap, chuppah, archway) are all amazing options to frame the ceremony. This gorgeous mandap captured by Kelsee Becker Photography is one of my all time favorites.

All of these items will be visual focal points of the ceremony and reception. Your guests will be spending a significant amount of time staring at these items throughout the event, so the extra effort and money you invested in the style will be noticed and appreciated. These are also areas that are easier to maintain throughout the event, so they will still be photo-worthy hours into the day.

On the flip side, I would not recommend over-styling the following aspects of the wedding because they will not provide a good return for all the effort, time and money invested:

Gift/Card Table

Keep things simple with a card box or basket or birdcage and let it go. There are always a few guests who bring a poorly wrapped present and set it smack dab in the center of a perfectly designed gift table. This reality will be very frustrating if your guests are "ruining" your picture-perfect display.

Guest's Tables

Overstyling the guests' tables can actually make the room seem overpacked. Your guests need elbow room and will be much more comfortable if they can actually have space to eat on the dining table. Keep space on the guest tables open. Remember, the table fills up fast with phones, purses, beverages, and food.

Escort Card Table

For some finding their escort card might be a challenge already due to bad vision or too much fun at the cocktail hour. It is best not to add to the challenge with an overly busy seating card table. Inevitably, the escort cards will be moved into a chaotic mess by your guests as they look for their names. If you want thing looking perfect at all moments, consider an alternative option. Lots of couples are opting for a seating chart sign and those can add more style and fullness to a space, as well as staying neat and tidy at all times. Whichever approach you take, *always group names in alphabetical order*, not in table number groupings, as it will help people find themselves faster.

Photo Booth Table

If you are including a photo booth at your wedding with all the silly props, don't even try to style the prop table. Havoc will be unleashed on that table as guests cycle through. This table is a workspace. Take a breath and let it go.

Water Table

This is another area that should be considered a workstation. Select a spot that is out of sight or can be tidied up often by staff as this area can become a soggy mess.

Ceremony Aisle

You can certainly add some florals displays, potted plants or decor items along the aisle. I recommend using items that can be reused after the ceremony to the reception site. Be careful to not to block the guests' view with huge displays or create a tripping hazard. It is best to avoid glass items on the floor (lanterns, votives, etc.), as those are often kicked over accidentally by the time the ceremony wraps up. Those more delicate details are better suited to framing the ceremony.

Ceremony Entrance/Welcome Table

A little sign welcoming guests and some florals is all you need. Let the ceremony backdrop be the centerpiece of the venue. Allow guests to have one clear focal point as they explore the ceremony site.

Guest Chairs

Rather than investing in trying the hide some old tattered chairs from the 1970s, just secure nicer chairs that blend with your style. Rental companies offer chair covers and bows which clutter the room. When you factor in the cost of the old chairs, chair covers, and bows, you'll likely find that nicer chairs are often the same price. To save money on chairs, arrange for the wedding party or some strong volunteers to relocate chairs from the ceremony to the reception site. If you have a vision for some over-the-top, decorative chairs, use them for the sweetheart table only.

Considering the specifics of your venue, the event layout and other visual focal points on site, you may find that you want to include fewer design touches. For example, if gorgeous architectural details are on site to frame your ceremony, you really do not need to add additional flowers or votives. You want to create fullness, warmth, and style with your stylish touches without over-styling and wasting precious dollars.

One under-appreciated and surprisingly affordable design feature that adds massive drama and style to any space is lighting. Market, fairy, or string lights, as well as uplights significantly add to the mood of an event, particularly weddings in the twilight hours. Many venues already have some lighting built into the venue or available for a small fee.

Borrowing string lights from friends and family (be sure to label them so you can return them after). If you have access to the venue in advance, setting up the lighting yourself is a very simple DIY. If you can not secure lights to borrow, then consider purchasing lights and reselling them after the event. If you decide to rent lighting secure them from a company like DIY Uplighting. They provide detailed setup instructions, cover all shipping costs and avoids upcharges for break down in the middle of the night.

If you are trying to style your wedding like a pro on a tight budget, the best plan of attack is skipping the rental company altogether. Incorporate items you have available for free! This seems obvious but is so very often overlooked. Do you or does someone you know of a home decorated in alignment with your wedding vibe? Borrow items to add to the wedding style. It can give your event the look you are aiming for without the cost and incorporates your loved ones in the day.

For your vintage wedding, borrow your relatives' china and crystal. Label each item, so you get them all returned after the event. They will likely be honored and happy to have their items showcased on your special day. Frames, vases, small decor items, table settings and more are likely available for free; they may be stashed away in a relative's garage or dining cabinet. Reflect on who had a wedding or celebration recently and might have a bunch of items boxed up in their closet. Ask nicely and let people know that it would mean a lot to you to involve their special items in your celebration.

Real Wedding Case Study

⌒⌒⌒

Jodi and Adam

Oct 20, 2018

Lake Balboa, CA

⌒⌒⌒

Jodi and Adam were aiming to keep their wedding day low stress, affordable, and representative of their creative style. Jodi said she used their one and a half year engagement to research and watch for deals.

Selecting a friend's beautiful home as their venue set the foundation for a cost-effective celebration. The amazing friends used the upcoming nuptials as motivation to finish some upgrades they had been delaying in their yard. There was also an artist's studio on the property with a large mural in the works which added to the fun and funky style of the event.

Jodi did not prioritize florals, so her and a few friends handled those as a DIY project. She also took advantage of a "going out of business" sale of a local fabric store to stock up on fabrics and ribbons to add to the style.

They were very fortunate to have a number of friends help make the day special and affordable. She said there was no shortage of people willing to support making their day amazing by contributing homemade desserts, building the chuppah, and adding fabric drapery to some indoor spaces.

If she were to do it again, she would really focus on releasing any anxiousness or worries about the event. Her nervousness a specific vendor distracted her from fun at times and were all for nothing since the whole event came together flawlessly.

If you can not find a specific item you need within your personal network, you can put an ask out on social media. Connecting with old friends to crowdsource resources is an easy task on Facebook or Instagram. If you do not feel comfortable asking people you know for help or guidance, there are tons of other resources.

There is an amazing group on Facebook called *Buy Nothing (Your Town)* which are local groups all over the US. It is a community of people who are happy to give or loan items to others in their neighborhood. Join the group and watch for items you need or ask for something specific. It is an eco-conscious and budget-friendly sharing community that I encourage couples to explore (for your wedding and life in general).

Other fantastic groups on Facebook are called *Something Borrowed, Something New* and *The Bridechilla Community*. These groups include vendors, recently married couples and brides/grooms to be. Search on Facebook and you will find these groups or similar groups in your local area. What I love about these group is that everyone comes together to support each other and couples on all budgets can find solutions that suit them. It is a hub of support, referrals, and ideas for those in the planning stage, as well as a little marketplace for all sorts of used wedding items.

Any items you can't source for free, aim to find gently used online or locally. Consider buying linens, votives, signage and other decor items with the intention to resell them after your big day. There are many sites that cater to reselling wedding decor including Tradesy, Wedding Recycle, Bridal Garage Sales, and Bravo Bride. These are amazing resources for securing items and unloading them after your beautiful day passes.

If you are hoping to resell items, take a few steps to maximize your cash back opportunity. Avoid over-personalizing things. Rather than including your names or the wedding date on the welcome sign, keep it simple. See the gorgeous "Welcome to our wedding day" sign from Etsy crafters like Chalk in Hand.

Keep the majority of tablecloths simple, as they are easier to resell and more affordable to have cleaned. Go with the more expensive, unique linens only on a few of the tables. For example, if you were envisioning sequin tablecloths, use those on the sweetheart table and cake table with more simple complimentary linens on other tables.

Any items you plan on reselling should remain unaltered. If you are adding custom details, attach them in a way where they can be removed easily without damaging the item. Keep the colors neutral on items you hope to resell; if you have a color pallet with bold or unusual wedding colors, find ways to incorporate them in items you plan on keeping. Of course, you can also consider borrowing or renting these items.

Renting items is rarely the most budget option. It is the EASIEST option, but you are paying a premium for the convenience. For example, if you compare ninety-inch round ivory rental linens from one of San Diego's major rental company with buying linens via Smarty Had a Party. Buying the linens is $1.25 per table cheaper on the list price, both companies would offer discounts to bring down the total down a little bit. Shipping/delivery is where the savings is big; free shipping to purchase the linens versus $100 minimum delivery fee (depending on the location and order size). When you factor in the ability to resell the linens, you are looking to save about fifty percent when you buy rather than rent.

If you prefer rentals for the convenience, aim to avoid the expensive delivery fees. You can save by selecting a reputable online rental company, like Rent My Wedding or BBJ Linens, who will cover the shipping both directions or find a small, local rental company and handle delivery yourself to negotiate a better deal. Whichever you choose, make sure you *return all items you rented* to avoid big penalties for damaged or missing items.

Did you know rental companies often make their best margins on broken and lost items they rent out? The fees for a lost or a damaged item can often be so significant that you could have purchased the items several times over. Delivery and pick up fees often cost far more than couples might imagine. Venues generally want all the rental items removed immediately following the event and rental companies charge a supplemental fee for the late night pick up in addition to the standard delivery charges. With all the fees and order minimums, even a small order can balloon into a large expense.

Each incremental bit you save on decor for your big day will add up faster than most imagine. Because you can collect, store and resell most decor items, you have many opportunities to develop the vision for your day as the event approaches. Making the choice to invest time and energy rather than dollars can allow a couple to pull together a gorgeous celebration without overspending.

Floral Sweetness

A room full of beautiful and aromatic flower does add so much romance and luxury to a wedding celebration. When you are working within a budget, florals are often one expense category to suffer a huge hit because the quotes from florists simply scare couples away from including these beauties at all. It is exhausting to search for vendors and disheartening to be told your budget is too small to work with. As with all other aspects of a budget wedding, when you get creative and put in a little extra effort, you can find the perfect solutions. Whether you decide to take on florals yourself, bring in a pro, or divide and conquer, this section will outline many budget-minded recommendations and tips.

My most important advice is to approach florals with a very flexible vision. Rather than focusing on a specific flower, focus on the feeling, color pallet, and style you'd like the florals to add to the event. This will give you or your florist flexibility to find great solutions that are in-season and on budget. If you love peonies and hoped to fill the room with them at your November wedding, you must understand the expense for flying fresh flowers in from the other side of the world will likely not suit your budget. You'll need to be flexible and open to other ways to approach this challenge.

For those who plan to forego a professional florist to handle flowers as a DIY project, be aware that fresh floral arrangements are a more advanced DIY project. The reason florals are a challenging DIY wedding project is two fold:

1. Fresh florals are extremely time sensitive. You can not prepare fresh arrangements far in advance; this is a task that needs to be completed within hours of the wedding. Often, this creates a much higher level of stress for all involved and may suck the fun out of a day that should be relaxed and full of joy. Depending on your personality, the savings may not be worth it.

2. The raw materials, fresh flowers, are expensive. If you purchase flowers to create your own arrangements and something goes off track, it will be a costly mistake that is hard to correct before the wedding.

Unless you have experience with floral arrangements or have a friend or family member who is well trained and willing to assist you, I would not recommend taking on *all* florals as a DIY project. My general recommendations are to have a professional handle a floral altar, any large statement pieces and personals to minimize stress near the wedding day.

For the couples who are up for the DIY floral challenge or those on a razor-thin floral budget, Costco Warehouse or Sam's Club may be a great option. Both warehouse stores offer some amazing but limited wedding flowers options—personals, table runners and bulk flowers are all available. They lack variety but provide some solid staples which can be used as a based for DIY arrangements. The collections of personals are a very reasonable option, but may not suit everyone's taste. They are certainly a great value for the couple who has florals low on their list of priorities since the process is very low stress.

If you select to arrange your own flowers, aim to work with very sturdy flowers. Without the skilled hands of a seasoned professional, you can easily damage delicate flowers. Stick with varieties that hold up best like protea, alstroemeria, mums, and daisies. If Costco doesn't have the varieties you'd like in stock, you can order flowers from sites like Blooms in a Box or Fifty Flowers for a very reasonable price. Unfortunately, browsing the flower market days before your wedding is likely a time luxury you will not have, so source florals in a convenient and cost-effective way.

For DIY, consider mixing in silk flowers or wood flowers, so you can have some arrangements prepared in advance. Creating the personals (bouquet, corsage, and boutonniere) in advance with silk flowers can minimize the workload hours before the wedding. Succulent arrangements are a great option for your DIY arrangements and are currently very on trend. Succulents can be prepared much further in advance and can double as gifts for special guests.

After the wedding, succulents can be re-planted in your garden and make lovely home decor. There are many professional florists specializing in succulents as well. Succulently Urban in San Diego can prepare and ship wedding complete arrangements and bouquets anywhere in the US; they also provide DIY succulent resources like pre-wired succulents, training, and other helpful tools. The cost of succulent pieces may not be far less than florals, but you can enjoy these arrangements and plants for much longer. Here is an example of one of Succulently Urban's bridal bouquets captured by True Photography.

Another trend that is very popular and saving some couples money is opting for more greenery and fewer blooms. You can bring texture and life to the arrangements with lots of greenery and pops of flowers. Eucalyptus, pepper tree leaves, fern leaves, pine and palm fronds can all make full arrangements or beautiful table runners.

It is important to note greenery is only slightly more cost effective if you need to *purchase* it; it becomes *significantly* more affordable if you can forage supplies from your yard, a park or elsewhere. Here is a great tutorial on preparing a greenery garland table runner. The process is a lot more labor intensive than just laying leaves on the table. If you are not totally in love with the style of heavy greenery and you are only opting for this style just to save money, there are likely easier options for the same price.

An example of a very simple, affordable and lovely style to consider is potted plants. Filling the event in with live plants instead of fresh-cut flower arrangements wherever possible can result in a huge time and cost savings.

Potted plants work well for the escort card table, guestbook table, and adding fullness around the ceremony or sweetheart table. There are a ton of examples here. Pothos, fiddle leaf fig, snake plant, orchids, ferns, and lilies are beautiful and stylish; these plants can cost pennies to the dollar compared to fresh flower arrangements and will add life and fullness to the room. You could add life to a table with a gorgeous potted plant for $20 rather than $100-200 for a professionally arranged floral centerpiece. To maximize savings, you can check with small, local nurseries about "renting" these plants from their stock for a weekend—they make some extra money, no flowers were harmed and your event had loads of style.

Rather than putting a pricey floral arrangement on both sides of the aisle, why not set some live topiaries for a pop of color? Small shrubs or trees can be a great option to consider around the altar and sweethearts table. You can plant them in your yard after the wedding as a memento of your special day or arrange for a weekend rental from a nursery. You will be surprised to find that there are more opportunities to add the fullness of flowers and plants to your day without following the traditional route.

One amazing tech-based platform is saving couples money by leveraging technology to partner up on wedding floral costs. This site connects two local couples who can share floral displays and save money. Flowers from a Friday night wedding can be freshened up and reused on Saturday night across town. Professional florists work with you to customize the arrangements to your needs, refresh florals so they look gorgeous for both events and handle transportation between events.

Couples can save ten to sixty percent on fresh flower arrangements with Bloomerent.com. **Use promo code *Heather* and save $50 off your florals on Bloomerent.** Everyone saves money without losing any style and florists get to show off their work to more party-goers.

Couples can also approach florists with the negotiation techniques outlined earlier in this book to create a win-win deal for themselves and the vendor. There is no reason to limit the beauty and style of your event due to your budget, with a little resourcefulness and effort anything is possible.

Calligraphy, Paper and Other Lovely Details

In the Pinterest and Instagram era, the pretty little details have really taken center stage with regard to the vision many have for their wedding day. There are some very talented people out there making handmade, custom pieces for couples and they are unbelievably talented. If the look of your event is a high priority and you have the budget to get some custom invitations suite made for your wedding, I would recommend Twinkle & Toast . Their work and creative vision are incredible. For those who are not able to spend $2,500 on a dreamy invitation suite, you will certainly enjoy their work for style inspiration.

If you are working on a more limited budget for your paper goods, then you will be able to find something a little less custom, but no doubt lovely over at Minted, Costco or Basic Invite. These sites both offer pre-designed invitations, save the dates and more to suit all styles. There are self-printing options available for those who might have access to local discount printing. Before you send your order to the printer, remember to double check the number of invitations that you need, often couples print too many. If you are inviting one hundred guests, you may only order forty to fifty printed invitations since most invites will be sent to a couple or family.

If you are blessed with the artistic skills to create your own invitations, then designing and printing invites yourself is an affordable option. I would recommend running a test print for a small batch to confirm the paper, design and print quality all look perfect before making your big order for all the invitations.

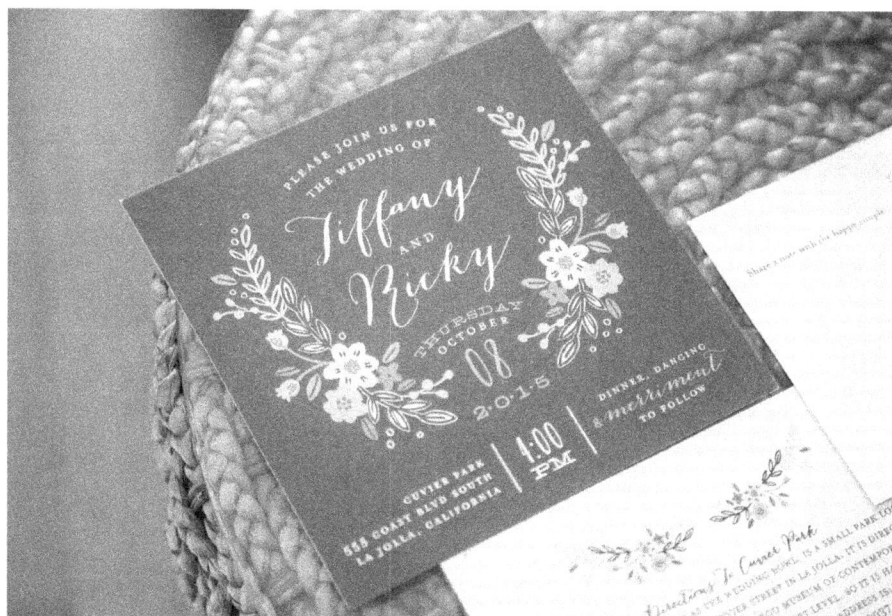

Favors, escort cards, place cards, menus, and programs can all be beautiful touches to round out the event design. Sometimes including all of these can be a heavy burden on a wedding budget. Lots of couples are opting for one large seating chart sign in lieu of escort cards for larger wedding receptions. Sign templates are available on Etsy and can be printed at your local print shop. With a beautiful frame, a sign can add more style and fullness to the room. Just make sure to *group names in alphabetical order*, not in table number groupings, as it will help people find themselves faster. Signs outlining the program and the menu are also often more affordable for a large wedding.

One item that often seems extravagant when on a budget are wedding favors; it is a tradition started by aristocrats as a display of gratitude to the guests for attending the celebration. The tradition of providing a small treat as a wedding favors is long-standing, but many couples aim to be creative and reflect their taste and sensibilities with the small gifts. My personal recommendation is to use this opportunity to make a contribution close to your heart. You can announce to your guests during the reception that in lieu of a favor, $x per guest was donated to a charity of your choice. The donation to a charity is a lot more significant and honors your guests in a way that is long lasting; making that announcement also adds a little excitement to the event and provides a tax write off to you.

Beyond the favors, it is common for couples to provide a gift to each member of their wedding party. Personally, I find surprising your wedding party with a special experience is more significant than a wine glass with your wedding date etched into it. If you do prefer something physical, purchase something your friends will actually use and enjoy regularly. My favorite gifts that I have received when serving as a bridesmaid were a lovely necklace and a beautiful robe —both of which I am still using years later. Be practical and really think about what your friends will enjoy.

Out of town guests are sometimes provided a little gift to welcome them to town. I think it is a thoughtful gesture, particularly if guests have traveled a great distance and are unfamiliar with the area. You don't need to spend a lot on this gift. It is all about the gesture, so a few cookies from a local bakery and a sweet handwritten note will be enough to warm the hearts of the weary traveler arriving for your celebration.

On the same note, gratitude is a must when planning a wedding. Attending a wedding, being in a wedding, working at a wedding can all be very exhausting at times. Your guests, wedding party and vendors have all planned their day (and likely whole weekend) around celebrating you and your spouse. Express gratitude whenever possible. Keep an organized list of gifts you receive, so that you can promptly send out thank you notes after the wedding. Thank you notes are not optional; to save on costs you can certainly send out emails, but sending a physical thank you is always best. Plan on sending thank you notes within six weeks of the wedding. You will likely have gifts arrive before the wedding, so consider writing a few notes each week as gifts arrive to avoid a backlog. Showing gratitude never goes out of style.

Dressed and Ready to Wed!

This is one expense with huge potential to balloon. Price tags can range from zero to many thousands of dollars for all items within this category. Everyone wants to feel good on their special day. Finding an outfit that makes you feel beautiful is very important. There are many ways to achieve this and there is no need to spend a million dollars to feel like a million bucks on your wedding day.

Remember that part of wedding tradition is to have "something borrowed". Wearing grandma's pearl earrings, your mom's refashioned wedding gown or your best friend's wedding veil are all amazing options to include a special borrowed item. Incorporating items from those you love is so meaningful. If you make your request to borrow an item in a loving manner, it will feel like an honor rather than an inconvenience to those you include in this way.

With the current vintage wedding style that is popular, reinventing a vintage wedding dress from a mother figure can be a great, cost-effective option to consider. Rather than buying a new dress with no personal significance, you can make something that is yours from a family heirloom. That is a very beautiful and special thing.

Re-invigorating a vintage dress will be particularly affordable if you or another family member is a skilled seamstress. For those who do not have the skills to handle updating the dress, hiring a professional seamstress can be expensive. Be sure to get a clear estimate on cost and timing before getting started. If making use of your grandmother's wedding dress is something you would love but the dress is in bad condition or not your style, perhaps there is a way to integrate part of the dress into your veil or another accessory.

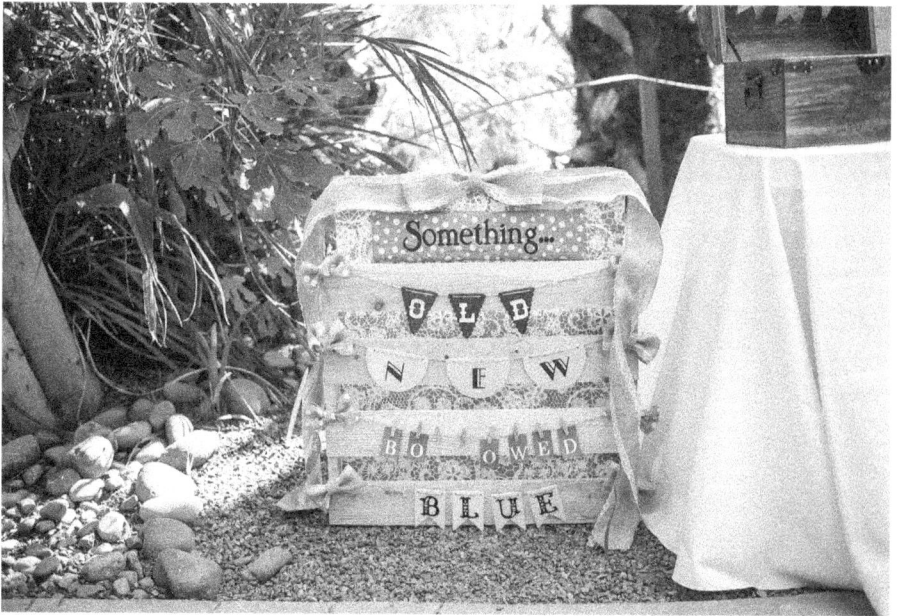

If you do not have access to a dress to make your own at no cost, then your next best option is buying a used dress or sample sale dress. There are many online resources for buying used gowns and many towns have a local shop that specializes in used or vintage dresses. Some great online resources for preowned dresses are NearlyNewlywed and Tradesy. You can often find dresses for thirty percent of their original price! Tapping your personal network is another option, perhaps you have an old friend or relative who recently got married and would be willing to sell their dress; some people are very attached to holding on to their wedding dress, but a large number of brides decide to sell their dresses and make space in their closets.

If you imagine yourself in a new and trendy dress, there is hope for you to find your dream dress on a small budget. Without the overhead of the retail space and staff, you can often purchase the same dress at a deep discount online. First, browse your local traditional bridal shops, try on dresses, take photos, make notes, and find something to suit you. With a clear vision in your mind, go home and check online shops.

The store staff will likely encourage you to hurry your decision and order because shipping can take months. Shipping and alterations do take time, but you certainly have time for a few days or weeks of online reconnaissance. Take a breath, relax, and take your time. Dress shops generally have unforgiving return policies, so you want to be certain before making a purchase.

Personally, after browsing a local shop to investigate pricing and style preferences, I bought my wedding dress from a sample sale website for about ten percent of the listed retail price. My dress only cost me $150 including shipping; the price tag stated $1,500. I spent about $200 on a few minor alterations and a steam clean before our wedding day. Be confident! There are amazing deals out there.

Just because you are buying online does not mean you have to miss out on the shopping experience. Go out to a shop to try on dress styles with your friends and family. For many brides, having so many opinions and people involved is stressful, so remember that you are not obligated to include a huge group. If you find a dress in a shop that suits your budget and style, amazing. You can get the dress or look into a layaway program if that is a better financial fit. You will want to confirm the timing for delivery of the dress since some bridal shops take much longer than others.

Another cost to weigh in the equation is tailoring, cleaning, and preservation. It is not uncommon for brides to spend $1,000-2,000 on dress tailoring, cleaning, and preservation. With this in mind, try to get a style that fits your needs rather than customizing a lot of details. Depending on the number of adjustments, you can quickly spend more on a seamstress than you did on the dress itself. If you are struggling to locate your dress in the perfect size, check a size up. It is far easier and more affordable to "take in" a dress rather than squeeze into a small dress or try to "let out" a dress.

One affordable online resources for dresses that has stellar reviews from brides is CocoMelody. As with any online purchase, I recommend reading the reviews and understanding the return policies before ordering.

For brides who are marrying a service member or first responder (or are one), I encourage you to investigate Brides Across America which provides free wedding dresses to those serving our country and community.

Interested in an awesome dress and helping the world at the same time? The online gown resources listed below have gorgeous, affordably priced gowns that also help great causes. Once your wedding is over, you have the option to keep, resell or donate your dress to share the love.

Here are some resources for buying, selling, and donating wedding gowns:

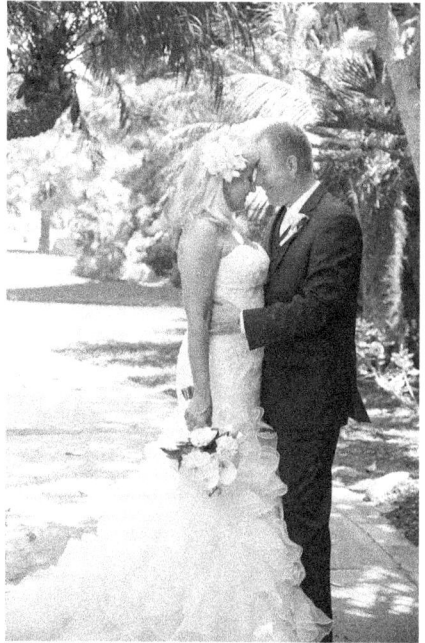

Brides for a Cause: Supports varied charities each year
Brides Against Breast Cancer: Supports breast cancer research
Mary Madeline Project: Creates burial gowns for stillborn babies from wedding dresses
Adorned in Grace: Fights sex trafficking with proceeds from gowns sold
Fairytale Brides: Supports varied women's charities

As far as wedding day accessories, I see this as a great opportunity to get creative rather than buying something new. If you have your heart set on something in particular… so be it, it is your day! Do your best to purchase new items that have a chance of being worn again in your normal life or being resold. Rather than purchasing shoes that only make sense with a wedding gown, perhaps pick something fun and funky that goes with your normal "going out on the town" attire.

Personally, I purchase some Grecian goddess style gold flats for my wedding day and I wore them until the soles fell off. My husband and I even had a little goodbye ceremony when I finally let them go years later. Depending on the venue, wardrobe, weather, and style of your wedding, any shoe will work for a wedding. I've seen books, sneakers, sandals, stilettos, and everything in between, so pick what feels right to you.

Regarding a suit, tux, and other accessories, it is almost always more economical to invest in a suit and get it tailored than to rent. Over the long term, the investment into a suit will save big; it can be used for other weddings and events with a simple change in accessories. Watch for a sale and have a vision of what style and color you are wanting before you start shopping.

If you do not foresee a suit being a good investment for you, then research your local rental shops. Often, shops will offer a free rental to the groom when there are X number of groomsmen rentals. Give everyone plenty of time to schedule their fittings. If you have friends flying in for your celebration, many shops like Friar Tux Shop and Men's Warehouse allow fittings at any location in their network, so it will make things convenient for all. You can always dress up the rental suits with some customized touches. Fun, colorful socks, pocket squares or suspenders can add some flair to the look and serve as a nice little gift for the groomsmen too.

On your wedding day, you want to feel and look your best which is why many times a glam squad is hired to help with hair and makeup. Depending on what your vision is for your wedding day look and your comfort level with makeup and hair this might not be needed. I am not particularly confident in my hair styling or make-up skills, so splurging on a pro was a huge stress reliever. I was also fortunate to have a future aunt-in-law who is a professional hair stylist; she insisted on getting me ready for the big day. It was a wonderful gift from her, fun way to involve her in the wedding festivities and saved me the stress of sourcing a hair stylist.

Tapping your network for glam help is always my first recommendation. Styling a bride on her wedding day can feel too high pressure for some people. If no one in your circle is open to being your glam squad, do not be upset. Another option is to ask a professional in your circle to teach you how to create the look yourself. Take some of the pressure off by having a practice styling session weeks before the big day and learn the process for your wedding day look. If you spend some money stocking up on quality hair and makeup products, it will be a better long-term investment than having your styling done for a single day.

If the thought of doing your own wedding day makeup is just too stressful, my next budget-friendly suggestion would be to go visit your local makeup experts (ULTA, Sephora, Nordstroms, etc.) and get a makeover. Explain the look you are envisioning for your look and have someone glam you up. If you love their work, ask if they are available to do makeup on your wedding date. Note, if you mention that this is for "wedding makeup" the cost will go up. Schedule the appointment for a general makeover and you will save a bundle. Purchase some of the makeup used (something you'll use regularly or will be needed for touch-ups that day) and offer a tip to compensate the makeup artist.

For this to work, you'll need to go to the store the morning of your wedding for your appointment. Allow for plenty of travel time in your schedule and take your mother or maid of honor with you to make the outing a fun part of the day. With regard to hair, just like with makeup, going to the salon to get styled up will be more affordable than having the stylist coming to you. Depending on the look you want for your wedding day, you can schedule yourself for a blowout or a formal bridal hairstyling session. Just remember pricing will go up once you add the word "Bridal" or "wedding" in the mix.

Your wedding day will be filled with emotions and excitement, so you will probably not be in the mood to sit still and relax for an hour. With this in mind, do not try to squeeze in a spa day the morning of your wedding. Booking a relaxing couples massage for the day after your wedding is a much better plan to decompress after all the excitement. Other beauty treatment (facials, waxing, etc.) and any touch up to your hairstyle or color should be done at least a week before the big day. If you want an eyebrow touch up, plan that for a few days before the wedding, just in case a problem comes up. For the men, I recommend booking a trim a two to five days before the wedding for optimum, fresh style.

Wedding bands are one of the tiny detail that will be on center stage on your big day. These rings are symbolic of the love and are something to be treasured, but there is no need to spend a fortune on them. If an engagement ring did not come in a bridal set and a custom ring is needed, things can get very expensive. Rather than spending an enormous amount on a custom ring to fit perfectly with your engagement ring, consider your nine other fingers. You can wear a more affordable wedding band and enjoy your engagement ring on your other hand. Remember, that your wedding day is the start of your lifelong commitment, so if you decide in a few years that you want to get that custom wedding band made, you always can.

Reasonable options available for brides and grooms. Sourcing your wedding bands online is an affordable option and can save you the drive to a jeweler; there are many beautiful options on Overstock and Etsy. Titanium and tungsten rings have become hugely popular in recent years and are virtually indestructible; they are also very affordable and stylish. For those in the athletic circles, there has been a huge interest in silicone wedding bands which can be safely worn while lifting weights and working with heavy equipment. It is important to note that silicone, titanium and tungsten rings cannot be resized, so be sure you purchase them in the perfect size.

No matter what you wear on your big day, the top priority should be feeling comfortable so you can be in the moment, soaking up all the love and beauty around you. Keep perspective that it does not matter how much you spend on your wedding day look, so long as it makes you feel like a million bucks.

Bring on the Fun!

N othing gets the party going or drags it to the grinding halt like music and entertainment. Setting the right vibe for the event is critical to creating the experience you are aiming for. Depending on your taste, you may have specific music in mind; generally, the music starts out soft and more mellow throughout the ceremony, cocktail hour, meal and then builds up to a full-force dance party as the event progresses.

You can develop the soundtrack for your day with the help of a band, DJ or personally crafted playlist. Your priorities and budget, as well as the space available at your venue, will impact which of these options will be best for your celebration. No matter which you approach you take, your event can have the energy you want with a little planning.

The most costly option for wedding music is a live band. This option also takes up a significant amount of space within your venue. If you are in love with the idea of live music at your wedding but are short on space and cash, there are some options to integrate rather than a full band for the whole reception.

- Ceremony or cocktail hour music. Would an acoustic guitar, harp, or violin to accompany the ceremony and entertain guests before the ceremony suit your vision? This is another opportunity for change up in the music and bring the wow factor of a live performance at your wedding without the huge cost.

- Special performance. Do you have a friend or family member who loves to be on stage? Would they enjoy singing or performing a song live during the reception to add to the festivities? Do you have a cultural heritage that can be honored with a performance? Does your church have a choir or vocalist available to perform?

If you decide you want to go with a performer or band for the reception, be sure to use the list of questions on the coming page to ensure you are securing a reliable entertainer. There are many awesome websites for locating a great performer suited to your budget; Gigmasters.com or Thumbtack.com both allow you to receive bids from available vendors in your area and see reviews for past events. These are excellent resources for any wedding entertainment.

For the reception, having a DJ is generally more cost-effective than a band (unless you fly in a DJ from Ibiza). Experienced wedding DJs often serve as the master of ceremonies for the reception and will help keep the schedule moving along smoothly. If you provide the DJ (and other vendors)with a detailed plan of events for the reception, they can keep the event flowing without the help of an event planner or day of coordinator.

One concern for many couples is that some bands and DJs can be overly hoaky and goofy when on stage. They may include songs you do not care for in their standard wedding line up (Macarena anyone?). It is very important to cover all the bases by checking references before the event and communicating your music preferences.

Questions for your potential DJ:

1. Do they have testimonials and references to back up their work, and can you contact the references?

2. Will they spend extra time helping you plan your event in advance?

3. Can they read your crowd to get them up and dancing?

4. Do they listen and customize your event to your specifications?

5. Will the person you speak and meet with actually be your event DJ/MC?

6. Will they take care of all the necessary announcements, and how much experience do they have as an MC?

7. Do they have a large song library that covers all the genres and has clean lyrics?

8. Can you give them a music request list in advance?

9. Are they fully insured, and do they have a business license?

10. Do they provide backup equipment at every event?

11. Do they have footage of prior events you can see?

12. Do they understand your preferences in music and vibe? Are they able to align their energy, clothing, and performance to match your goals?

Assuming you want your reception to involve dancing, the selection of a DJ who knows how to get people on their feet is very important. To ensure the party energy fills the room, assign your outgoing friends and family the job of starting the dance party during the reception. As soon as the dance music comes on that is the cue to jump out on the floor without delay. Breaking the ice quickly is important and allows the more reluctant guests a little more confidence to get out on the floor. If the dance floor fills up on the first song, it is very likely that it will stay full all night long. If the floor is awkwardly empty for the first few songs, guests will start edging their way toward the doors to head home early.

Regarding the dance floor, some venues will have formal dance floors installed or available as a part of the venue rental fee, others will not. Depending on the flooring and venue rules, it may not be necessary to rent a dance floor. My opinion is if the floor is flat and solid, you can dance on it without a special dance floor. You can distinguish the dancing area with overhead lighting and by spacing the tables properly. No need to pay extra for a wooden floor to be delivered, set up and later broken down. If your venue requires a dance floor, be clear on the pricing for the delivery and breakdown within the venue's allowable delivery window. Often venues require that all vendors remove items within just a few hours and the rental company may charge extra to accommodate this.

The most budget-friendly option for entertainment is to borrow or rent a sound system, create a playlist for the event and get your outgoing (cousin, uncle, friend) to be the MC for the night. You will want to make detailed notes about which songs are to be played for key events during the reception: first dance, cake cutting, father-daughter dance, mother-son dance, honeymoon fund dance, etc. These same details must be provided to a professional DJ or band.

With an amateur MC at the helm, there is a little room for things to get off track, but overall, you can get the same experience for far less money. Your uncle saying something embarrassing about when he first met your spouse will likely just add to the fun and funny memories of the day.

Remember that a wedding is really just a party, so one of the most important goals is to make it fun. If you stick to you and your love's vision, you will be having fun and so will the bulk of your guests.

Real Wedding Case Study

Katy and Edinson

Aug 19, 2017

San Diego, CA

Katy and Edinson priorities were food, fun, their outfits, and photography. Katy expressed her focus on their relationship rather than the wedding, saying, "as long as we got married, at the end of the day, we were going to be happy."

They saved big by finding a reception venue that credited their venue fee toward the food and beverage expense. Minimal florals, upgraded online invitations, and using the venue's sound system with a playlist rather than hiring a pro all contributed to keeping the event on a budget.

Katy noted that if she did it again, she would take her couple photos on a day following the wedding to minimize stress and save more money. She also would have skipped cake altogether because so much went to waste. Expenses for dress alterations were one item that gave Katy sticker shock; she mentioned that brides should plan for alteration costs when selecting a dress.

She also reiterated that couples should avoid getting sucked into the wedding industry marketing machine which pressures you to spend big and keep focused on your relationship.

Capturing the Memories

Before digging into photography, which is most often the highest priority vendors for couples, ask yourself…

How important are wedding photos to you now? How about in ten, twenty-five, or fifty years?

Now, ask your parents, grandparents, or another older friend or relative about their wedding photographs. Almost all of them will tell you that they treasure the photos they have from their wedding day; most will also mention that it has been many, many years since they last looked at any of these photographs (except for the few framed in their home).

Only in recent years, did it become commonplace to have hundreds, or even thousands, of photographs from a single wedding day. We are so accustomed to this convenience that we forget that only a few decades ago, photography was totally different for weddings. We now have the ability and expectation that we capture every single moment of our wedding day. I have seen photographers tell couples that they could *never* get all the photos the couple *need* in only four or six hours. Is that really true? In a few years, just like your elders, you will have a few framed photos in your home and the rest will be in storage. Your wedding photographs are certainly precious keepsakes, but be realistic in how many photographs you really *need* to remember the day clearly.

My biggest recommendation for your wedding day photography is to develop a list of all the special people who you would like a photograph with. Do not rush making this list and provide it to the photographer at the start of the day. Looking back on the day, you will likely find the photos on this list, as well as the photos of you and your spouse, are the only photos you really *needed*.

For those who truly love photography and feel that they must have every moment professionally captured, be prepared to make room in your budget by dialing back in other aspects of the event. Couples are often surprised to learn that wedding photographers come with a hefty price tag; photographers are doing far more than you see on the day of the wedding. They spend numerous hours editing photos for every hour they are on-site shooting and they are experts at their craft, so their rate is well deserved. Excellent and experienced wedding photographers cost anywhere from several thousand to tens of thousands of dollars for a full day of shooting.

If you are splurging on a professional,

- Review examples of full, real weddings in their portfolio, not just highlights or inspiration photo shoots

- Request full rights to your images, so you can print photos yourself at a lower cost at your leisure.

- Book the hours you really need the photographer on site only and develop the day's schedule to maximize the photographer's time

- Alert friends and relative that you will include in photos of the photo schedule, so you can be efficient

Depending on how you prioritize photos, you may decide to invest in photography and dial back in other areas to balance the budget. For those with some flexibility in their expectations for photography, there are ways to maximize what you spend on photography by considering some alternative plans.

One way to save big without sacrificing amazing couple photos is to book a portrait session with a top local photographer on a day following your wedding. Rather than paying a premium and constricting your wedding day schedule by packing in a full portrait session between the ceremony and reception, just leave those photos for another day. Every photographer's rate is much lower when you are not booking them for a full day of shooting at a very high-stress event.

If you are flexible and willing to get dressed up in your wedding look a second time, this plan will save you seventy to eighty percent on your wedding photos. Without the rush and stress, you may even get better photos since you will both be more relaxed. You will still get beautiful photos to commemorate your marriage but will save big on cost and will free up time on your wedding day to allow for more fun and time with your guest.

Of course, you will still need to make arrangements to capture the special people and key moments of your wedding day. With the portrait session booked for another day, you can aim to hire a photographer willing to work just a few hours on your wedding day. You will want them to arrive about thirty minutes before the ceremony and stay around for some family and friend groupings immediately following the ceremony. If the ceremony and reception are on the same site, you can also have the photographer snap a few quick photographs of the decor if that is important to you. Most couples agree that photos of their family, closest friends, and their newlywed portraits are the most treasured photos from their wedding day; with that in mind, have a professional capture just most important photographs and let your family and friends capture the shenanigans at the reception.

If your budget is super limited or photography is less of a priority for you, consider hiring an amateur photographer and /or videographer (maybe a friend or relative with a nice camera) to capture some photos and videos of your families, friends, decor and the ceremony. These photos will be lower quality than a professional, but you will have the memories captured to look back on in the future. If you are wondering where to locate an amateur or up-and-coming photographer consider Bark.com, Gigmasters.com, Thumbtack.com, Craigslist.com. On all of these platforms, you can list your maximum budget for your project, so even if you have a severely limited budget, you can post an ad for free and see if anyone is open to the opportunity.

BLUE 22 PHOTOGRAPHY

When you post your ad, I would not mention the word *"wedding"*. Including that word in the ad will potentially scare away some photographers getting their start. Any more experienced photographers will see that word in your ad and their price will go way up. Honestly, this is something to keep in mind with *all* vendor ads you place. The word *"wedding"* means HIGH PRESSURE to the vendor. You can prioritize your budget by making the day low key and dropping the wedding day stress. Keep your chill with vendors; you are opting for the financial savings and sacrificing the professional polish, so be understanding if there are some little bumps along the way. If your secure an amazing deal with an amateur vendor, be kind and do not morph into a bridezilla. Let the vendor learn from your wedding, understand that you may sacrifice a little refinement so that you can enjoy the financial savings.

Here is a template you can use for placing an ad for an amateur photographer for your event:

"We are looking for a photographer/videographer to capture a family event coming up on (date) in (city) from (hours you want them on site). We would love to have some photos/footage of the day, mostly candid and a few family photos. We are open to students or hobbyists and have a maximum budget of ($$$). We would like rights to all photos, so we can print them at our leisure. After the event, we would like all photos shared with us via (digital file sharing platform of your choice) within (x) weeks of the event. Please email us your quote for the event hours, any examples of your work."

With this approach, I have gotten photographers to work several events for as low as about $50 per hours. Remember, that the photographer will have to spend time organizing, uploading and sharing the photos with you after the event, so they will be spending some time after the event ends to finish up the project. The photographer may or may not get a bit frustrated or nervous when they realize the event is a wedding. Just reassure them that your goal is for them to capture candid photos and you are realistic in your expectations. After they finish taking photos, provide a generous gratuity for their cooperation.

If even an amateur photographer is out of your budget, then your next best option is to crowdsource your photos and video. Create a wedding hashtag on social media, so all the images from the event can be found in one spot. Or better yet, get apps like Eversnap and Wedit turn a few of your guests into your photographers and videographers. With everyone capturing the event from different angles, it is likely that you will end up with your memories beautifully captured.

Over the last decade, photo booths have become extremely popular at weddings. They make for a fun activity for guests to enjoy and result in lots of funny photos for your scrapbook. There are many great companies out there who can host a photo booth station, but you can also opt for a more affordable DIY option. Rent My Wedding offers a professional DIY photo booth kit shipped to you without the hassle or cost of managing another vendor. You can get creative with the photo booth backdrop and props for your guests. This DIY option will allow you to have the splurge of a photo booth without spending much at all.

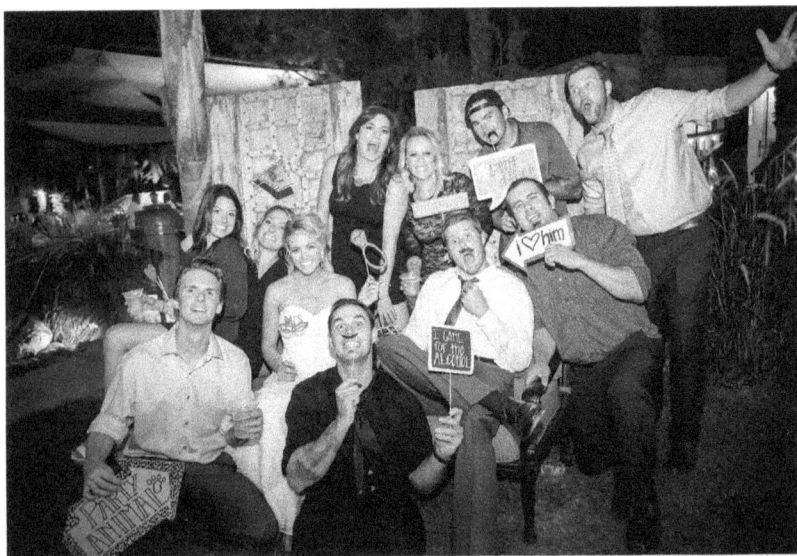

No matter how much or how little you are able to spend on your photography, there are resources out there that can make capturing your day possible. You are investing a lot of time, energy and money into your special day, so enjoy it and capture the memories along the way.

Riding *and* Parking *in* Style

If you are holding your wedding ceremony and reception at two different locations, transportation for yourself, the bridal party and potentially the wedding guests can get complicated. Many times wedding parties rent a limousine to handle transportation between the ceremony and reception, as well as back to the hotel after the reception. The problem with this is most limo services will have a minimum rental period and you will be paying for the driver and the limo for many hours while it sits outside of the reception.

When you are on a budget, this just feels like a waste. Of course, if a limo was on the top of your priorities for the event, then please go ahead and get one booked. My recommendation would be to allow your wedding party to arrange for their own transportation; they might have significant others or a family needing some of their attention, so driving themselves will give them a chance to check in between their duties as a part of the wedding.

If you'd like to do something extra special for your vehicle after the ceremony, renting a car on Turo for the day or the weekend. You can cruise between events in a luxury sports car, a rare vintage vehicle or some other dream car for far less than the cost of a full day limo rental. If you are concerned that you will not be capable of driving by the end of the night, look into a luxury car rental group, like Luxe Car Collective in San Diego to handle the driving and the car rental; Luxe has gorgeous cars like a Tesla Model S and Maserati available to transport you between your ceremony and reception or reception and hotel in style. Rather than paying for a limo to sit in a parking lot, you'll pay half the price for a much more exciting ride. If you have a friend or relative who owns a classic or exotic car, perhaps they would be willing to drive you and show off their "baby" on your wedding day.

Another potentially complicated issue is parking at a venue. The general rule for parking is to ensure there is a reasonable, affordable option for your guests. It is not the couple's responsibility to provide free parking, so long as some parking is accessible within a reasonable distance to the venue. Do keep in mind elderly guests or guests with small children attending the event who might be especially challenged by having to park far away and walk to the venue. If parking will be challenging to guests or requires special arrangements, such as taking a shuttle or long walk, this information should be provided via the wedding website or within the invitation materials.

I've worked with venues that come with absolutely no parking and have terrible public parking nearby; the couple was forced to rent a parking lot for their guests and hire a shuttle service to transport their guests from the lot to their venue. This was a much larger expense than the couple anticipated and a complicated situation to manage. If you are on a tight budget, I would advise you to strike any venues requiring a shuttle and private parking lot off your list.

If the venue you are working with has paid parking or valet parking options, you can explore the possibility of paying for that cost on behalf of your guests at a bulk rate. This is not something you need to feel obligated to provide but is certainly a nice touch if you are able to accommodate it. If guests will be expected to pay for parking upon arrival, I would be clear about this on the wedding website or invitation insert. Catching your guests by surprise with an unexpected cash expense is a bad start to their evening. If you are prioritizing your guests' experience of your wedding, then small details like parking are worth considering.

Making it Official

O f all the wedding costs, there are only a few that are completely mandatory to make a marriage official: a county marriage license and an officiant fee or donation. If you or your spouse decide to change your name, then there will also be a few costs associated with that, as well as a little time.

You will want to check with your local county recorder/clerk's office to get details on the exact costs and timeline for securing a marriage license in your area. Often, you will need to schedule an appointment for a weekday during business hours that you and your future spouse can attend together. You will likely need some identification, such as a birth certificate and ID card.

The cost for the license is generally under $100 and you will have an option for a public or confidential marriage license. A confidential marriage license is not recorded in the public records, so only the married couple can access copies of the license from the recorder's office. The county office will often offer wedding ceremonies on site, although the available days and times may vary. If you are having a ceremony outside of the county office you will need your license with you on the day of the ceremony, so the officiant and witnesses (for a public license) can sign the document.

You want the ceremony to hold true to you and your spouse, so it is important that the officiant is a good fit for you both. Here are some questions to consider when researching officiants:

- Do you want a religious or non-religious ceremony?

- Do you want to participate in pre-marriage counseling?

- What values do you want your officiant to hold? Are you in alignment?

- Do you want to get to know your officiant on a personal level?

- What is your budget for an officiant?

- Reflect on wedding ceremonies you have attended, what did you like or dislike?

How you answer each of these questions will reveal what type of officiant will best suit your wedding ceremony. Finding an officiant can be a challenge for many couples; if a couple comes from different cultural or religious backgrounds, the couple may need to develop a completely unique ceremony merging traditions. Finding someone to carry out the unique ceremony that you envision will take some time and require interviewing several potential officiants. The officiant's personality and vibe should fit with couple flawlessly to allow the ceremony to feel most relaxed. Start your search for an officiant early in the planning process; the ceremony can really only start coming together once the officiant is selected.

Officiant fees vary widely between $100-500, but the average rate is about $250. If you are a member of a congregation, you can often secure the pastor for a donation to the church. For those that are not associated with a church, you can easily secure an officiant (religious or not) through vendor databases like Thumbtack.com, Bark.com or Gigmaster.com. Crowdsourcing, tapping your database for recommendations, is a great option to develop a short list of candidates to interview. Officiants are often eager to develop a ceremony with the couple to ensure what is special about the couple shines through.

In recent years, more couples opt to have a friend or family member officiate the ceremony. If you have a friend or family member who would be comfortable leading the ceremony, this is certainly an affordable option to consider. This is a lovely way involve and honor someone who has been significant in your relationship. There are a few websites that allow anyone to get ordained for free, such as American Marriage Ministries and Universal Life Church or for a nominal fee, such as Open Ministry.

Once the joyous ceremony and celebration are wrapped up, there is still a bit of paperwork to do if anyone will be changing a legal name. All the documents and paperwork are certainly not romantic, but getting the logistics handled so you can fully make it official is part of the process. Fortunately, the costs are minimal for the bureaucratic changes; there is even a service via HitchSwitch that can handle a bureaucratic headache for you, saving hours of time for a small fee.

Once all the paperwork is filed, you and your love can bask in the newlywed glow and celebrate being officially hitched.

Wedding Planning and Coordination

"Wedding planning" and "wedding coordination" are often used interchangeably, but refer to two different processes. "Planning" happens in advance of the event and includes dialing in the timeline, securing vendors, organizing logistics and guiding the style and vision of the event. "Coordinating" is the execution of the plan already in place on the day of the event, monitoring the vendors, crowd control, and cueing the flow of events. These two roles go hand in hand.

Most often "day of" coordinators handle some light planning in the weeks or month prior to the event. The reason this happens is that a solid planning before the wedding day is actually more integral to the flow of the day than the on-site coordination. If a coordinator jumps in on the event day with no prior preparations, the event will likely be burdened with chaos. Whereas when the planning is done very well before an event, the coordination on the day of the event is far more simple. The coordinator is on site as a safety net. Many times the safety net is not used, but everyone involved feels much more secure having it in place, just in case.

Having the coordinator on site allows the couple to feel confident that any problems that come up will be resolved and the day will flow smoothly. While working as a wedding coordinator, despite my clearest directions, timetables, and sitemap, I could not prevent certain issues from happening. Once a pastor mistyped the venue address her GPS, the typo sent her far off course and nearly delayed the ceremony. I have battled tropical storm force winds during an outdoor reception and helped clean up the dance floor after a bride tossed her bouquet into a chandelier and broke it. Despite thorough planning, I was unable to prevent any of these situations. I was there to help pick up the pieces, clean up the mess, and buffer the stress for the couple—that is what a day of coordinator is able to assist with. Serving as the wedding coordinator, I was able to take action to correct these issues immediately without involving the couple in the stress.

Some venues provide a complementary event manager and it is not uncommon for couples to misinterpret this as a wedding coordinator. A venue event manager is overseeing the venue's staff, equipment, and facilities. Most often this venue staff person is not available to offer their full attention to the wedding in the way that a dedicated coordinator would. Their focus is orchestrating the event from the venue perspective; managing the other vendors on site and the flow of the events are not their responsibilities. Often venues will require a wedding coordinator to be on site because it is understood that this is a very different role.

Day of wedding coordination is like insurance for the couple. It minimizes the mental stress and allows the couple and family to feel relaxed on their wedding day, knowing there is someone to handle any unexpected challenges during the day. Depending on your nature, you may be completely fine without a planner or coordinator. I would never tell a couple it is impossible to plan or coordinate a wedding yourself because that is a blatant lie. You can absolutely do it yourself. I have seen many couples have fantastic weddings without a planner or coordinator. About a decade ago, I planned and coordinated my own wedding without a single problem, but it is in my nature. I am very organized, good under pressure, and had a substantial amount of experience running events. For me, the thought of hiring a coordinator never even crossed my mind.

If your nature leans toward anxious, nervous, or easily stressed, or if staying organized is not your strong suit, you should absolutely bring on planning and coordination support. Working with a wedding planner to develop a very clear event timeline and communicate that plan to vendors is most critical. Once the framework is solidly built, you are able to recruit an organized and calm friend or acquaintance to handle the day of coordination. With a detailed timetable in hand, venue maps, and clear directions, many people are capable of serving as the wedding day safety net. Most couples have a capable, organized friend or acquaintance willing to volunteer (or work for a minimal amount) to serve as their wedding coordinator. The challenge couples face is finding an affordable event planner to bring the wedding day plan together and to provide the structure to the novice coordinator.

If you have a friend-of-a-friend who has the right personality and is willing to serve as your wedding coordinator, take advantage of this huge cost saving opportunity. Some professionals will insist this is "too risky". I suggest you ask that professional planner how they got their start in the wedding business. A vast majority of professionals get started by planning their own wedding or helping with a friend's wedding. Being a solid wedding day coordinator just requires an organized, calm personality and the right information, tools, and guidance.

The average day of wedding coordinators cost $1,500 and full-service wedding planning costs between $5,000 and $10,000. The reality of a budget wedding is that hiring a professional wedding planner or coordinator may feel like a luxury you cannot afford. Some venue will require the couple to hire a coordinator so couples are forced to fit this large expense into an already tight budget.

With budget-minded couples in mind, I developed a cost-effective solution for couples wanting the reassurance and support of a wedding planner without the enormous expense. This unique wedding planner support program called The Wedding Hacker Planning Club. For a low monthly cost, you can have access to unlimited professional support, a monthly one-on-one call and a wealth of helpful resources to help keep your planning on point.

You can relax because a pro is checking your work and available to guide you and support you. All the planners are trained in the wedding hacker ways, so they can help you develop creative solutions to overcome the hurdles you face along the road to your special day. Couples can enjoy a professionally polished wedding day timeline, personal attention, and exceptionally clear vendor communication without the full-service planning price. We can provide budget-minded referrals to vendors suited to your vision.

The Wedding Hacker also offers a BYOC (Bring Your Own Coordinator) program for friends or relatives who are willing to serve as an on-site coordinator. For a fraction of the price of a traditional day of coordinator, a couple can access the expertise of professional throughout their planning process and the reassurance of having a trained coordinator on site. Additionally, this program is able to advise you on securing the needed insurance documentation that most venues require, so that your aunt, cousin, or friend's sister can serve as your coordinator without any liability on the venue or the couple.

Making room in your wedding budget for wedding day coordination support is a decision that will allow you and your future spouse to be guests at your own wedding. No matter your preferences on the style, feel, and flavor of your wedding, this decision allows you to prioritize your own enjoyment of your wedding day. You deserve to be relaxed and enjoying every minute of the celebration you have been dreaming of.

Of course, if your budget is super slim, there are tools available to hack together a gorgeous wedding day timeline on your own. One resource that is used by professional planners is Timeline Genius; with a little time and effort, you can create a very detailed wedding day timeline in this slick system.

Going through their process, you will likely be alerted of many tiny wedding day details that you haven't considered yet. Will you have a first look? Will the cake cutting happen before or after the first dance? How much time will the bridal party need to travel between venues? These and many other details of the flow of your wedding day can be dialed in through this software. To develop the event layout and venue diagrams, you will want to tap a free resource like Social Tables. For a couple on the full-force DIY planning track, these softwares are lifesavers.

For the DIY couples, there is one other resource that may help you keep your sanity while staying on track throughout the months of planning. Bridechilla offers several amazing planning guidebooks which offer grounding support for the couple in the throes of planning a wedding. I am a big believer in the F.I.B. (check out the podcast to learn more). Releasing the yourself from the expectations that society, our families, friends and we put on ourselves is a huge step in creating an enjoyable wedding celebration. If you don't release all the expectations that are not important, you will likely miss the things that really do matter in the chaos of it all.

If your budget does not allow any room for additional support, there is one final suggestion. Tap the heck out of free online resources. There are so many excellent podcasts, online support groups, and blogs providing resources. As you cruise the internet looking for ideas and support, just remember, sometimes free items come at an unlisted cost.

If a company is not directly selling something to you (their own product or service), then *you* may actually *be* the product. These sites most often make money off of advertising products and services to you. This is not necessarily a bad thing. People running these resources work hard curating content, so they deserve to make some money. With their business model in mind it is always advisable to spend a little extra time to read some independent reviews (like Yelp) and dig a little deeper into the product or service before pressing the "buy now" button.

No matter your budget, there are ways to bring together your event in an organized fashion. As with all the wedding hacks, you may have to invest a little more of your own time to meet your budget goals. When investing the time feels like a drag, just focus on your excitement for your new marriage and love for your spouse, family, and friends. Your wedding day will be a day will be a special memory for all of the people you love, so whether you are investing money or time, the investment will be worthwhile. Happy planning!

Elopements, Pop Ups, and Surprise Weddings

For those of you who are looking to get down the aisle with the lowest cost and stress, I am going to run through a list of very nontraditional, adventurous and spontaneous approaches to a crazy affordable wedding. All of these options assume you have a very small guest list and align with the vision of an elopement more than a traditional wedding. By avoiding the traditional format of a wedding, the obligations and rules fall away; you are free to keep the aspects of a wedding that you personally value.

I will note that any of these can be done in tandem with a post-wedding celebration to include more friends and family to commemorate the special moment. I have seen couples hold very unique parties to celebrate their marriage from a potluck picnic to a bonfire on the beach. When you buck tradition, you open the doors to something totally unique and significant to you. These are ideas to get your creative thought process going in a direction that calls to your heart, suits your budget and allows for a stress-free celebration.

Flash Wedding!

Have you had your eyes on a beautiful venue, but the cost is too restrictive for your budget or way too large for the intimate wedding you envision. You want to have a small ceremony on the patio of the restaurant you ate at on your first date, in your favorite park, our outside of a gorgeous museum. Consider an outside of the box approach of a flash wedding. Invite a small group of guests (under twenty) to arrive, stand and watch a brief ceremony and then meet up elsewhere for a celebratory meal.

The pros are low stress, high excitement, more flexibility on venue and timing. The cons are a chance of being sent away by a security guard and minimal formality. Researching the location in depth to decide how to handle the impromptu event. Contacting the venue to get approval on your plan is a good idea if you are targeting a small business like your favorite coffee shop, wine tasting room or brewery. The owner or manager will likely be excited about the special, flash event. With only a small group of guests, the event will add a little extra excitement for the shop. For public spaces—beaches museums and parks likelihood of security intervening in your ceremony may be much lower and a local city permit might be available at a nominal fee to dial back any concerns.

Pop-Up Wedding!

Similar to the flash wedding in certain aspects, this is a stylized and professionally organized elopement. Pop-up weddings are orchestrated by a group of vendors, so they are beautifully styled and include all the key people you need to get a mini wedding experience. Top notch vendors set up a stunning backdrop and you show up, tie the knot and celebrate without the fuss of planning.

The pop-up wedding packages include everything you need and is perfect for the couple who is not interested in investing their time and money into a traditional wedding experience. Pop the Knot is one company specializing in this type of event in a handful of major cities coast to coast; they are pulling together some gorgeous styled elopement ceremonies for $1,000-3,000. The price includes coordination, venue, flowers, up to twenty-five guests, officiant, and photographer.

Surprise Wedding!

Invite friends and family over for an engagement celebration and surprise them by having an officiant present to make it official. Once all the guests have arrived, make a toast and announce that you are starting your married life together today!

Without the drama of a drawn-out engagement with lots of opinions offered, you will avoid a lot of complications of the day and make a very memorable celebration for your closest friends and family. Arrange for a photographer or nice camera to be handy, so that you can capture the moment. You can schedule a professional portrait session for the day after you've made it official to commemorate the occasion. Another twist on this surprise wedding is turning a styled shoot into a real wedding. I love the story of this couple's beautiful and romantic surprise elopement captured by Monique Serra Photography.

Wilderness Wedding!

Are you an outdoorsy couple who enjoys hiking and camping, why not have a ceremony off the grid? You can reserve a few of your favorite campsites and invite your friends to spend a weekend celebrating in nature with you. Hike up to a beautiful viewpoint for the ceremony and it will certainly be a moment that everyone will remember. Bring some blankets for cozy ceremony seating and stock up on food to cook up with your friends and family. Enjoy s'mores in place of cake by the bonfire.

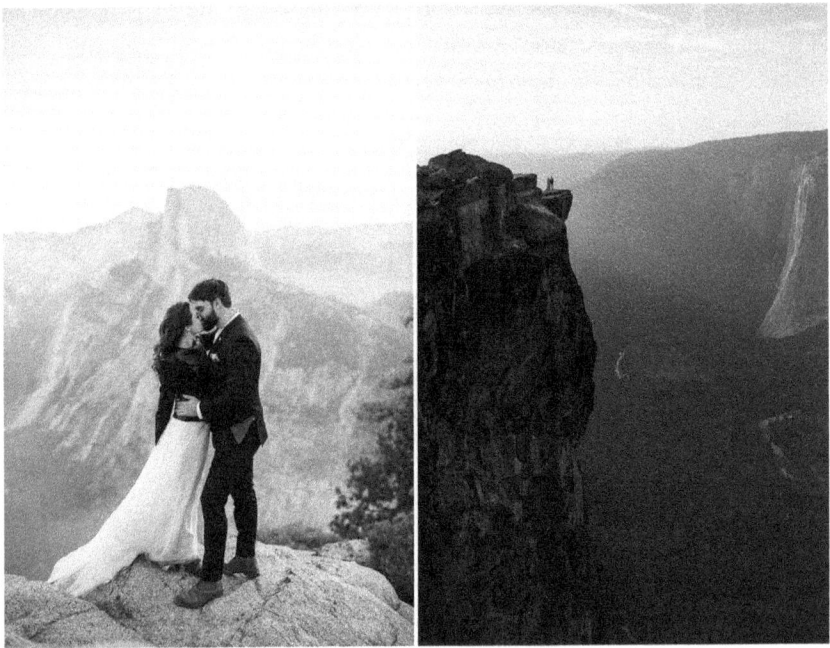

You'll want to arrange for a photographer specializing in epic adventure photography to capture the moment. The Hearnes Adventure Photography provides some amazing examples of how stunning, romantic and intimate these ceremonies can be. The elopement ceremony photography package is not particularly budget-friendly, but you can book a photo shoot to commemorate the day at a much more affordable price point… and, oh my, those photos will be stunning.

Your wedding day is meant to commemorate your love and commitment to each other—the way you choose to do that can be as beautifully unique as you and your love. There is no reason to hold tight to traditions that do not appeal to you and are stressing your budget. There is no reason to be weighed down by obligations and expectations of what your day will be. Your family and friends love you and want you to be happy; this means that they will understand if your wedding day is something that is different than they expect or perhaps doesn't involve them.

Reflect on what is truly important to you and your future spouse and do not apologize for following that. Remember to come from a place of love when letting your family and friends know about your elopement plans. Express to them that this is what best represents your love and vision for your celebration of this union; if they are at first frustrated, they will let it go over time. If you begrudgingly hold a large wedding to please others, it will not feel true for you and you will hold resentment toward those obligations each time you make a credit card payment. Make your day beautiful and make your day yours; whatever that means to you is just perfect.

Visit TheWeddingHacker.com/resources
for an current list of resources.

The Wedding Hacker

About the Author

Heather Loree Fier, aka the Wedding Hacker, has orchestrated tens of thousands of events across the US for private and corporate clients. While she has fun planning events with mega-budgets, Heather's passion is supporting couples in starting their marriage without a mound of debt. Finding creative and collaborative solutions to make a wedding happen on or below budget is what Heather loves.

Helping couples break free from the structure, tradition, and feelings of obligation associated with their wedding day is at the heart of *The Wedding Hacker* mission. Her advice to couples planning their wedding is to not lose sight of the most important part of your wedding day—your joyous commitment to one another.

When she is not planning events, Heather enjoys time with her husband, Joe, her dogs, and her foster babies. Since 2017, Heather and Joe have cared for six foster babies who were all under three years old; they are very passionate about improving the foster care system so that the amazing little ones have the opportunities in life they deserve.